ALLSENSORS 2023

The Eighth International Conference on Advances in Sensors, Actuators, Metering and Sensing

April 24th – 28th, 2023

Venice, Italy

ALLSENSORS 2023 Editors

Paulo E. Cruvinel, Embrapa Instrumentation, Brazil

Printed from e-media with permission by:

Curran Associates, Inc.
57 Morehouse Lane
Red Hook, NY 12571

Some format issues inherent in the e-media version may also appear in this print version.

International Academy, Research, and Industry Association (IARIA)
412 Derby Way
Wilmington, DE 19810

Phone: (408) 893-6407
Fax: (408) 527-6351

petre@iaria.org

Additional copies of this publication are available from:

Curran Associates, Inc.
57 Morehouse Lane
Red Hook, NY 12571 USA
Phone: 845-758-0400
Fax: 845-758-2633
Email: curran@proceedings.com
Web: www.proceedings.com

Table of Contents

ALLSENSORS 2023

Forward

The Eighteenth International Conference on Advances in Sensors, Actuators, Metering and Sensing (ALLSENSORS 2023), held in Venice, Italy, April 24 - 28, 2023, covered related topics on theory practice and applications of sensor devices, techniques, data acquisition and processing, and on wired and wireless sensors and sensor networks.

Sensor networks and sensor-based systems support many applications today above ground. Underwater operations and applications are quite limited by comparison. Most applications refer to remotely controlled submersibles and wide-area data collection systems at a coarse granularity. Other remote sensing domains and applications are using special sensing devices and services. Transducers and actuators complement the monitoring and control and constitute an area of interest related to sensors. They make use of specific sensor-based measurements and convey appropriate control actions.

ALLSENSORS 2023 was intended to serve as a forum for researchers from the academia and the industry, professionals, standard developers, policy makers, investors and practitioners to present their recent results, to exchange ideas, and to establish new partnerships and collaborations. The accepted papers covered a large spectrum of topics on techniques and applications, best practices, awareness and experiences as well as future trends and needs (both in research and practice) related to all aspects of sensor-based applications and services.

We take here the opportunity to warmly thank all the members of the ALLSENSORS 2023 technical program committee as well as the numerous reviewers. The creation of such a broad and high quality conference program would not have been possible without their involvement. We also kindly thank all the authors that dedicated much of their time and efforts to contribute to the ALLSENSORS 2023. We truly believe that thanks to all these efforts, the final conference program consists of top quality contributions.

This event could also not have been a reality without the support of many individuals, organizations and sponsors. In addition, we also gratefully thank the members of the ALLSENSORS 2023 organizing committee for their help in handling the logistics and for their work that is making this professional meeting a success.

We hope the ALLSENSORS 2023 was a successful international forum for the exchange of ideas and results between academia and industry and to promote further progress on the topics of sensors. We also hope that Venice provided a pleasant environment during the conference and everyone saved some time for exploring this beautiful city

ALLSENSORS 2023 Chairs

ALLSENSORS Steering Committee
Michael Niedermayer, Berliner Hochschule für Technik (BHT), Germany
Paulo E. Cruvinel, Embrapa Instrumentation, Brazil
Matteo Tonezzer, CNR-IMEM, Trento, Italy
Almudena Rivadeneyra, Universidad de Granada, Spain
Sandrine Bernardini, Aix Marseille University, France

ALLSENSORS 2023 Publicity Chair

Laura Garcia, Universitat Politècnica de València (UPV), Spain
Javier Rocher Morant, Universitat Politecnica de Valencia, Spain

ALLSENSORS 2023

COMMITTEE

ALLSENSORS Steering Committee

Michael Niedermayer, Berliner Hochschule für Technik (BHT), Germany
Paulo E. Cruvinel, Embrapa Instrumentation, Brazil
Matteo Tonezzer, CNR-IMEM, Trento, Italy
Almudena Rivadeneyra, Universidad de Granada, Spain
Sandrine Bernardini, Aix Marseille University, France

ALLSENSORS 2023 Publicity Chairs

Javier Rocher Morant, Universitat Politecnica de Valencia, Spain
Laura Garcia, Universitat Politecnica de Valencia, Spain

ALLSENSORS 2023 Technical Program Committee

Francesco Aggogeri, University of Brescia, Italy
Otman Aghzout, National School of Applied Sciences of Tetouan, Morocco
Amin Al-Habaibeh, Nottingham Trent University, UK
Youssef N. Altherwy, Imperial College London, UK
Darius Andriukaitis, Kaunas University of Technology, Lithuania
Piotr Artiemjew, University of Warmia and Mazury, Poland
Farzad Asgarian, University of Michigan, Ann Arbor, USA
Herve Aubert, Laboratory for Analysis and Architecture of Systems (LAAS-CNRS), France
Roberto Beghi, Università degli Studi di Milano, Italy
Artur Bejger, Maritime University of Szczecin, Poland
Roc Berenguer Pérez, TECNUN - Technological Campus of the University of Navarra, Spain
Sandrine Bernardini, Aix Marseille University, France
Mourad Bezzeghoud, University of Évora, Portugal
Xavier Boddaert, Mines Saint Etienne | Centre Microélectronique de Provence (CMP), France
Muhammad Ali Butt, Warsaw University of Technology, Poland
Ismail Butun, Chalmers University of Technology, Sweden
Maria Candelaria Hernandez Goya, Universidad de La Laguna, Spain
Juan Vicente Capella Hernández, Universitat Politècnica de València, Spain
Vítor Carvalho, 2AI-EST-IPCA / Algoritmi Research Centre - UM, Portugal
Paula María Castro Castro, Universidade da Coruña, Spain
Rosario Catelli, Institute for High Performance Computing and Networking (ICAR) - National Research Council (CNR), Italy
Debashish Chakravarty, IIT Khaargpur, India
Nan-Fu Chiu, National Taiwan Normal University,Taiwan
Susana Costa, University of Minho, Portugal
Paulo E. Cruvinel, Embrapa Instrumentation, Brazil
Luca Davoli, University of Parma, Italy
Marcos Antonio de Oliveira Junior, Federal University of Pelotas, Brazil
Francesco G. Della Corte, University of Napoli Federico II, Italy

D. R. Patil, Rani Laxmibai Mahavidyalaya Parola | North Maharashtra University, Jalgaon, India
Pablo Pérez García, Instituto de Microelectrónica de Sevilla, Spain
Vengadesh Periasamy, Low Dimensional Materials Research Centre (LDMRC) | Institute of Ocean, Earth and Sciences (IOES) | University of Malaya, Malaysia
Patrick Pons, CNRS-LAAS, Toulouse, France
Rüdiger Pryss, University of Würzburg, Germany
Parvaneh Rahimi, Institute of Electronic - and Sensor Materials | TU Bergakademie Freiberg, Germany
Reza Rashidi, State University of New York - Alfred State College, USA
Càndid Reig, University of Valencia, Spain
Almudena Rivadeneyra, University of Granada, Spain
Alexandra Rivero García, Universidad de La Laguna, Spain
Christos Riziotis, National Hellenic Research Foundation, Greece
Bahram Djafari Rouhani, Université de Lille Sciences et Technologies, France
Gonzalo Sad, CIFASIS / CONICET / FCEIA | Universidad Nacional de Rosario, Argentina
Markus Santoso, University of Florida, USA
Iván Santos González, Universidad de La Laguna, Spain
Jagannathan Sarangapani, Missouri University of Science and Technology, USA
Sudipta Saha Shubha, University of Virginia, USA
Mu-Chun Su, National Central University, Taiwan
Nur Syazreen Ahmad, Universiti Sains Malaysia (USM), Malaysia
Roman Szewczyk, Warsaw University of Technology, Poland
Alessandro Tognetti, University of Pisa, Italy
Matteo Tonezzer, CNR-IMEM, Trento, Italy
Anish Chand Turlapaty, Indian Institute of Information Technology Sri City, Chittoor, India
Diego Vergara, Universidad Católica Santa Teresa De Jesús De Ávila, Spain
Sudip Vhaduri, Fordham University, USA
Manuel Vieira, CTS-ISEL, Portugal
Manuela Vieira, ISEL-IPL/CTS-UNINOVA, Portugal
Stefanos Vrochidis, Information Technologies Institute - CERTH, Greece
Guang Wang, Rutgers University, USA
Xianpeng Wang, Hainan University, China
Ulf Witkowski, South Westphalia University of Applied Sciences, Germany
Marcin Wozniak, Silesian University of Technology, Poland
Qingsong Xu, University of Macau, Macau, China
Murat Kaya Yapici, Sabanci University,Istanbul, Turkey
Sergey Yurish, Excelera, S. L. | IFSA, Spain
Kristina Žagar Soderžnik, Jožef Stefan Institute, Slovenia
Lan Zhang, AIST, Japan
Shichen Zhang, Michigan State University, USA
Jingjing Zheng, CISTER Research Centre, Portugal

Copyright Information

For your reference, this is the text governing the copyright release for material published by IARIA.

The copyright release is a transfer of publication rights, which allows IARIA and its partners to drive the dissemination of the published material. This allows IARIA to give articles increased visibility via distribution, inclusion in libraries, and arrangements for submission to indexes.

I, the undersigned, declare that the article is original, and that I represent the authors of this article in the copyright release matters. If this work has been done as work-for-hire, I have obtained all necessary clearances to execute a copyright release. I hereby irrevocably transfer exclusive copyright for this material to IARIA. I give IARIA permission or reproduce the work in any media format such as, but not limited to, print, digital, or electronic. I give IARIA permission to distribute the materials without restriction to any institutions or individuals. I give IARIA permission to submit the work for inclusion in article repositories as IARIA sees fit.

I, the undersigned, declare that to the best of my knowledge, the article is does not contain libelous or otherwise unlawful contents or invading the right of privacy or infringing on a proprietary right.

Following the copyright release, any circulated version of the article must bear the copyright notice and any header and footer information that IARIA applies to the published article.

IARIA grants royalty-free permission to the authors to disseminate the work, under the above provisions, for any academic, commercial, or industrial use. IARIA grants royalty-free permission to any individuals or institutions to make the article available electronically, online, or in print.

IARIA acknowledges that rights to any algorithm, process, procedure, apparatus, or articles of manufacture remain with the authors and their employers.

I, the undersigned, understand that IARIA will not be liable, in contract, tort (including, without limitation, negligence), pre-contract or other representations (other than fraudulent misrepresentations) or otherwise in connection with the publication of my work.

Exception to the above is made for work-for-hire performed while employed by the government. In that case, copyright to the material remains with the said government. The rightful owners (authors and government entity) grant unlimited and unrestricted permission to IARIA, IARIA's contractors, and IARIA's partners to further distribute the work.

Characterization of an IoT Stereo Image Sensor System for Weed Control

Bruno M. Moreno[1,2], Paulo E. Cruvinel[1,2]

[1] Embrapa Instrumentation (CNPDIA), P.O. Box 741, 13560-970, São Carlos, SP, Brazil
[2] Postgraduate Program in Computer Science, Federal University of São Carlos, São Carlos, SP, Brazil
Emails: bruno.moreno@estudante.ufscar.br; paulo.cruvinel@embrapa.br

***Abstract*—Smart farming has emerged as a new option to deal with the adversities of food generation in agriculture in the face of growing demand, with the aim of increasing productivity allied to the search for a more sustainable world. One of the objects of study in precision agriculture is weed control and the conscious use of inputs. This article presents the development and characterization of an embedded stereo system using camera sensors and Internet of Things principles, for future application in the area of digital image processing. Concepts of validation of lenses by Modular Transfer Function, calibration of intrinsic parameters of sensors and 3D system and memory and energy consumption management are analyzed, and implemented in the construction of an equipment, which aim to control invasive plants in crops.**

***Keywords*—camera sensor; stereo vision; embedded platform; weed control; agricultural industry.**

I. Introduction

Agriculture is a very important source of food, feed, fiber and even fuel. Despite this, agriculture currently faces the challenge of increasing its production in response to the demand of continued population growth, taking precautions against the various adversities caused by the climate and minimizing the impact of man on nature [1].

One of the approaches aimed at increasing productivity in the field is the reduction of losses due to factors exogenous to crops, such as competition resulting from the presence of invasive plants. The presence of weeds in the cultivation area can decrease crop yield by more than 50% just by competing with the moisture present in the soil, causing more damage than invasive animals, diseases and other pests [2]. Therefore, weed control is essential so that the nutrients present in the soil, the development space and the reception of sunlight remain exclusively for the plant of interest [3].

Moreno and Cruvinel presented previous studies related to a stereo camera's system [4], and the development of a software based on semantic computing concepts for the segmentation of weed plants [5].

Although the use of pesticides has already been established to deal with this problem, technological applications aimed at the rational use of inputs are desired. Among such technologies, Computer Vision stands out, which works in two stages: image acquisition and image processing. The acquisition is made exclusively from camera sensors, capturing the environment and patterns present in digital images. Such sensors can then capture the visible or thermal spectrum, and be coupled to vehicles, devices, robots, drones and even satellites. On the other hand, affordable single-board computers have made onboard image processing possible [6].

Image processing can be summarized in five steps. In the first, the raw data are pre-processed, removing noise and selecting only the object of interest. In another step, pattern features are extracted, whereas in the case of plant images, such parameters are related to color, shape and texture. In the third stage, the features go through a selection process, decreasing the dimensionality of the data. Afterwards, the data are classified, grouping them based on their similarities. Finally, in the decision making stage, new input data can be classified from the already trained model, thus identifying which group it belongs to [7][8].

To ensure that the input data are of good quality, validating and using good camera sensors have become extremely important. Allied to this, other points of consideration in the application of such techniques in agriculture are the management of the volume of data generated, the data analysis techniques that need to deliver interpretable and understandable results due to the interdisciplinarity of workers in the area, and the mobile systems that need to be able of handle scarce resources such as limited battery life, low computational power and limited bandwidths for data transfer [9].

As examples of the use of camera sensors in the field, there are applications coupled to vehicles to operate during pre-planting and analyze the height and density of vegetation from the images [10] and identify the location of invasive plants for manual control via weeding machine [11]. Plant images can also be acquired to create a database on an external server for further processing, for training a future classifier [12].

This paper is structured as follows. Section II presents the materials and methods used, including the Internet of Things (IoT) system description, camera sensor specifications, stereo vision basics, and embedded board specifications. Section III presents the results of the validation of the sensor and of the stereo system, the power supply and memory limitations and the final prototype, with the final conclusions in Section IV.

II. Materials and Methods

The developed system aims to capture stereoscopic images in a real environment of plantations, so that the presence and concentration of weeds present in the region of interest can be identified from an embedded algorithm. The capture of stereo images requires two camera sensors, generating two images of the same area that will be the input of the system. The images are then processed and grouped into classes, and the data will be prepared for sending to a module external to the system, which will be responsible for spraying the site.

A. High-level IoT architecture

Embedded systems have a potential in agricultural use due to their mobility, low cost and computational power, allowing the performance of complex tasks in a more practical way. Raspberry Pi (RPi) is being used in several applications and it is the leading candidate for hardware implementation due to its powerful processor, rich I/O interface and compatibility that allows most projects to run on it [13]. Its wireless communication also makes the RPi capable of working with IoT projects, allowing objects to be sensed or controlled remotely across existing network infrastructure and reducing human intervention [14].

IoT systems in agriculture are separated into three modules: farm side, server side and client side. The farm side usually consists of detecting local agricultural parameters, identifying the location and sensor data, transferring crop fields data for decision making, decision support and early risk analysis based on recent data, and action and control based on the monitoring of the crop [15]. As can be seen from the block diagram in Figure 1, the developed IoT Stereo System can gather image data in the field, pre-process, segment, create feature extraction and depth information vector, classificate and interpret the collected data, while being controlled and monitored via Bluetooth serial communication by a mobile app.

On the server side, the network layer is responsible for reliable transformation to the application layer. A Wireless Personal Area Networks (WPAN) network can be mounted on a single board computer, with its own unified control and monitoring console for various wireless networks. Data transport and storage become essential, with data that can be saved on an external server or in the cloud, and then transferred to other devices, including the equipment responsible for product spraying on the plantation. The last module, the client side or application layer, collects and processes information, providing an environment where users can monitor data processed by the system via a web browser, anywhere and anytime.

B. Embedded System and Camera Sensor Specifications

RPi is a series of mini-embedded computers developed in the United Kingdom by the Raspberry Pi Foundation in association with Broadcom. The model used was the RPi 3 B+, where its specifications can be seen in Table I. It is important to note that board must be powered with a nominal voltage of 5 V capable of delivering 2.5 A of current, with operating temperature between 0 °C and 50 °C. The internal memory is defined from a micro Secure Digital (SD) card, where the kernel of the operating system is also present, being recommended the use of at least 8 GB of memory. The RPi 3 B+, unlike previous family models, enables BCM43438 wireless Local Area Network (LAN) and Bluetooth Low Energy (BLE) communication, allowing wireless data exchange.

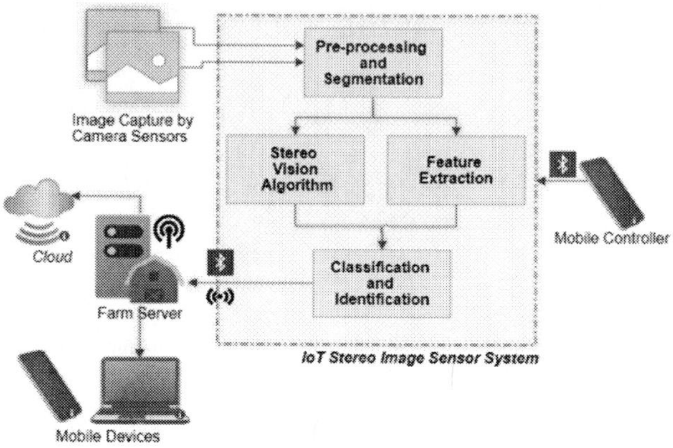

Figure 1. High-level system architecture diagram.

TABLE I
RASPBERRY PI 3 MODEL B+ CHARACTERISTICS

Processor	BCM2837B0 Cortex-A53 (ARMv8) 64-bit		
Clock	1.4 GHz	GPIO	40 pins
Memory	1 GB SDRAM	Gigabit Ethernet	1 connector
USB Port	4 USB 2.0	HDMI	1 connector
Camera serial interface (CSI)		Display serial interface (DSI)	
Wireless (dual band)		Bluetooth 4.2/BLE	
3,5mm 4 Jack output		Micro SD card slot	
Support Power-over-Ethernet		Input DC 5V/2.5A	

TABLE II
PI CAMERA CHARACTERISTICS

Size	25 x 24 x 9 mm
Resolution	5 MP
Video modules	1080p30, 720p60, 640x480p60/90
Sensor	OmniVision OV5647
Sensor resolution	2592 x 1944 pixels
Sensor image area	3.76 x 2.74 mm
Pixel size	1.4 μm x 1.4 μm
Optical size	1/4"
Full-frame SLR equivalent	35 mm
S/N Ratio	36 dB
Dynamic range	67 dB @ 8 times gain
Fixed focus	1 m - ∞
Focal length	3.60 ± 0.01 mm
Horizontal field of view (HFOV)	53.50° $\pm$ 0.13°
Vertical field of view (VFOV)	41.41° $\pm$ 0.11°
Focal ratio (F-stop)	2.9

The RPi has its own camera sensor alternatives, including the Pi Camera v1, with specs shown in Table II. Among the most important parameters, stand out the fixed focal length of 3.60 mm, the maximum sensor resolution of 2592 x 1944 pixels, and the camera opening angle of 53.50° horizontally and 41.41° vertically.

C. Modular Transfer Function as Camera Sensor Validation

The Modular Transfer Function (MTF) expresses how well an optical system preserves the contrast of spatial frequencies of the object in the image and is a well-established performance method [16]. A popular way to estimate the MTF curve for spatial frequency is called the inclined knife-edge method, in which the curve is obtained from a region of the image where there is a transition from a very dark tone to a very light tone [17]. An Edge Spread Function (ESF) is calculated from the recorded knife edge, giving the one-direction response of the imaging system to an edge object. The Line Spread Function (LSF) is obtained by the derivative of the ESF.

Then, the use of a camera sensor can be defined taking into account the calculation of the LSF of the camera lens and MTF, which represents the magnitude response of the optical system to sinusoids of different spatial frequencies, i.e., retrieved by Fourier transform of the LSF. Taking a linear source the solution to measure the MTF is in 1D, orthogonally to the direction of the line. This can be proven considering a given source $S(x,y) = \delta(x).C$, and a lens of diameter equal to a, that means:

$$R(k_x,k_y) = \int\int_{-a/2}^{a/2} \delta(x)Ce^{j(k_x x+k_y y)}dxdy \tag{1}$$

The response of the objective can be expressed as the square of the Fourier transform of the product of the source with the aperture of the lens $R^2(k_x,k_y)$, with (k_x,k_y) the spatial frequencies associated with the spatial coordinator (x,y). Besides, looking for a solution of (1) and solving the integral by parts is possible to reach:

$$R^2(k_x,k_y)\alpha\frac{sin^2(ak_y)}{(ak_y)^2} \tag{2}$$

Equation (2) corresponds to the LSF. The Fourier Transform of the LSF then gives the 1D MTF in the yy-direction. In stereo systems, usually the MTF system data are summarized as a curve for each sensor or just the curve of the lowest quality sensor [18]. Therefore, the images from the cameras are convolved based on the multiplication of their MTFs in the frequency domain.

D. Stereo Vision Principles

Stereo vision systems are usually based on the use of two cameras with the aim of simulating the human vision system and obtaining depth of objects, with the camera plane as a reference. The depth is acquired through the comparison of the object's position between each captured image [19]. The simplest way of comparing both images is guaranteed when the cameras are coplanar and aligned, as shown in Figure 2. The variables defined by the camera system are the baseline b and the focal distance f. The $P(X,Y,Z)$ represents a point that would be recorded by the two cameras and $u_L = (X_L, Y_L)$ and $u_R = (X_R, Y_R)$ are the projections of this point in each image. From the concepts of geometry and similarity of triangles, it is possible to obtain:

$$Z = \frac{bf}{X_L - X_R} = \frac{bf}{d} \tag{3}$$

The d variable is called disparity. Thus, with two images as inputs in a calibrated and synchronized stereo architecture, depth information is obtained by finding the corresponding pixels in both images (u_L and u_R) by a matching algorithm and subtracting their X-axis coordinates. By performing this operation for all paired pixels in the image, the disparity map

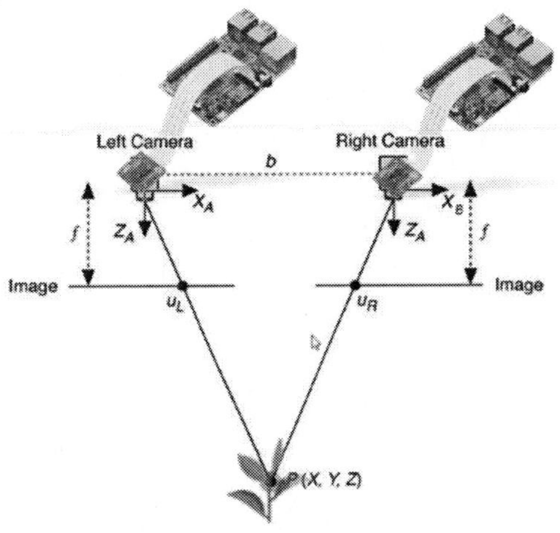

Figure 2. Stereo vision model.

is obtained, which contains all the depth information in the image.

It is also important to note the distortion that variations in the disparity map can cause in the depth estimation, i.e., verify the measurement obtained accuracy. So, for a variation in depth, it is possible to find:

$$\Delta Z = Z - \frac{bf}{d+\Delta d} = \frac{Z^2\Delta d}{bf + Z\Delta d} \approx \frac{Z^2\Delta d}{bf} \tag{4}$$

During image capture, the focal length f and baseline b are fixed, but the baseline distance can be adjusted to minimize this distortion, taking into account the expected distance of objects from the camera. Thereby, the system calibration can be done from an image of a chessboard on which its pattern allows to rotate and adjust the stereo images so that they are lined up and the difference between them is only in the horizontal dimension. Before calibrating the system, it is necessary to find the calibration of each camera, which is defined by two matrices, the camera matrix and the distortion matrix [20]–[22]. The camera matrix, presented in (5), is composed of intrinsic parameters as focal length f_x and f_y, and optical centers c_x and c_y. On the other hand, (6) shows the distortion matrix, where q_1, q_2 and q_3 represent the lens radial distortion coefficients and p_1 and p_2 the lens tangential distortion coefficients.

$$\textit{camera matrix} = \begin{bmatrix} f_x & 0 & c_x \\ 0 & f_y & c_y \\ 0 & 0 & 1 \end{bmatrix} \tag{5}$$

$$\textit{distortion coefficients} = \begin{bmatrix} q_1 & q_2 & p_1 & p_2 & q_3 \end{bmatrix} \tag{6}$$

Finally, the calibration of the entire stereo vision system can be summarized by (7), where $\mathbf{R_x}$ represents the rotation factor and $\mathbf{T_x}$ the translation factor between the captured left and right image [23][24].

$$\textit{Left Image} = \mathbf{R_x} * \textit{Right Image} + \mathbf{T_x} \tag{7}$$

Note that unlike the camera matrix and distortion coefficients which depend only on the camera, the $\mathbf{R_x}$ and $\mathbf{T_x}$ matrices must be recalculated if any stereo system settings change such as, for example, the baseline distance.

III. Results and Discussions

Experimental results were focused on the instrumentation' s characterization, i.e., including both the sensors and hardwares associated with signal and image processing. So far, the images for such a characterization were collected at laboratory level only. The system is based on eight elements, as follows: 12 V battery; 12 Vdc to 220 Vac voltage inverter; Light Emitting Diode (LED) lamp; 110-220 Vac to 5 Vdc rectifier; two RPis and two Camera Pi, as the schematic presented in Figure 3. All components are fixed on a metallic structure, with adjustable distance between cameras, angle of inclination (0º, 90º, 180º, 270º) and height of the cameras in relation to the ground (10 to 100 cm). The built system can be seen in Figure 4.

The system is controlled by an Android App via Bluetooth serial communication, where commands can be sent: synchronous image capture on the two RPis, send the images to the cell phone to check the quality of the capture, check the amount of images saved on memory, and board reboot or shutdown command. The RPis also communicate with each other via Bluetooth protocol, that supports up to 7 accessory devices, and uses Radio Frequency Communication (RFCOMM) Bluetooth protocol in data transfer with the cell phone. To ensure system security, it connects only to trusted equipment on specific ports.

A. Energy consumption management

A RPi can has power consumption of up to 12.5 W, but in laboratory tests the usual value during the application of the image capture software was only 3 W. As the system was designed with a inverter, the power consumed by this equipment must also be considered for system evaluation and possible improvements. In this case, the inverter in question presented a spent power of around 8.4 W, significantly higher than the sum of the RPis. To deal with such power, a battery of 12 V and 60 Ah was chosen.

To measure the energy expenditure of the system, current and power were calculated in different situations, according to Table III, with battery voltage fixed at 12.0 V. To evaluate the battery capacity, a test was carried out in the most extreme situation, with the system in continuous operation with the 18 W LED lamp on, which resulted in the maintenance of operation for approximately 15 hours. When the battery was discharged to 11.7 V, the inverter stopped as a safety precaution. It was observed that, in this operating mode, the peak current at system startup was close to 3.2 A, while with the same configuration but with the less potent LED lamp the peak was 2.0 A.

B. Memory management

For each RPi a 32 GB SD memory card was selected. After the initial settings, the necessary programs installed and the capture algorithm developed, about 23.1 GB of memory was free for general use. To ensure that the program can handle the amount of data written and stored, it is good to know how long the embedded system takes to save files. In testing, it was found that the SD card sequential memory write rate is 14833 KB/s or 14.8 MB/s.

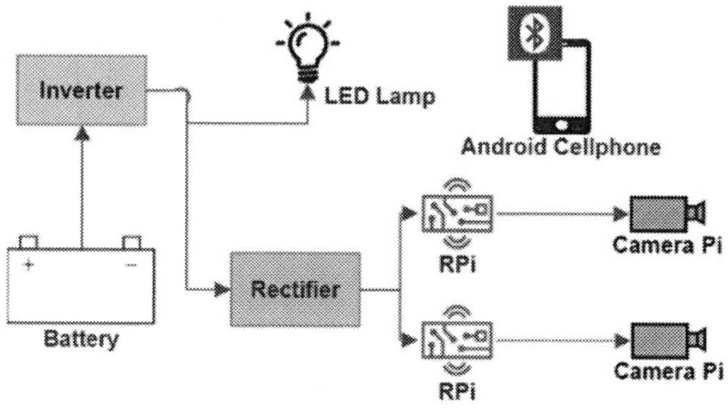

Figure 3. Diagram of the connection between the components.

(a) Details of the camera, stereo rig and lamp.

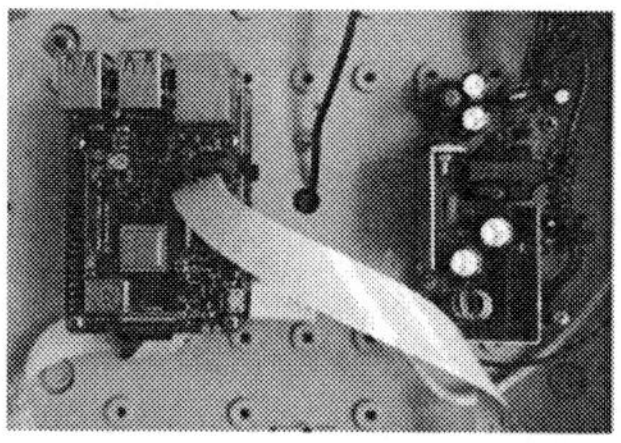

(b) Interior of protective case, with RPis and rectifier.

Figure 4. Developed system.

TABLE III
System Power At Different Settings

Mode of operation	Current (A)	Power (W)
Standard	1.3	15.6
With active camera sensors	1.4	16.8
With active camera sensors and 4.5 W LED lamp	1.9	22.8
With active camera sensors and 18 W LED lamp	3.0	36

Such information is important to define the resolution in which the images will be captured, as they define the size of the files saved in memory. Following the dimension of the camera sensor, it is preferable to define the resolution of the captured images to take advantage of the entire sensor size, that is, in which the 4:3 ratio is preserved. The maximum file size can be calculated by multiplying the resolution by the pixel depth, but since the Pi Camera doesn't have the option to format a RAW image file, the images are compressed, resulting in smaller files. So, it was tested five resolutions, 640 x 480, 800 x 600, 1024 x 768, 1280 x 960 and the maximum 2592 x 1944. Early test results can be seen on Figure 5, where five images in each resolution were taken and saved in the PNG format.

Considering the future application in image processing, in which the computational cost of operations tends to grow

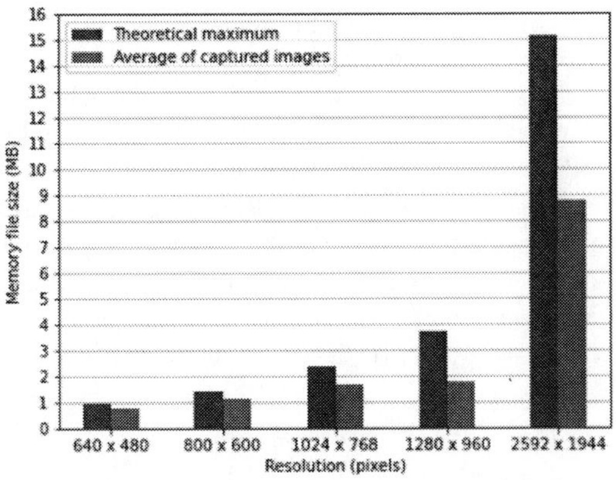

Figure 5. Image file size experimentations.

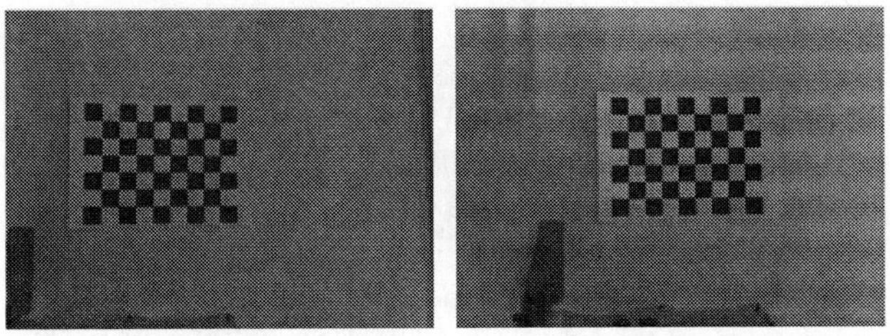

(a) Left Camera. (b) Right camera.

Figure 6. Images of a calibration chessboard, captured synchronously and without being processed.

exponentially according to the number of pixels present, and the available SD memory, the resolution of 1280 x 960 was then chosen. With this resolution, at least 6,000 images can be saved in memory, although it is possible to store them later in the cloud, from the system's communication with an external network, freeing up space on the board. It should be noted that for future applications, if the maximum resolution is used, the memory writing time must be taken into account as a limiting factor.

C. Camera sensor validation

The first step in calculating the stereo MTF was to capture an image of the chessboard with both cameras at the same time, as can be seen in Figure 6. For each image, five random regions were selected where there are knife edges recorded, in the same location for both cameras. The normalized MTF was calculated for each point and averaged between them, and after that, the MTF of the stereo system was then calculated from the multiplication of both MTFs, as can be seen in Figure 7. The MTF value at the Nyquist frequency was then 14.31% for the left camera, 8.97% for the right and 1.28% for the entire system.

To evaluate the camera's SNR ratio, only the regions of the converted grayscale image where black blocks were presented, which have a uniform color on the original chessboard, were used, and the mean and standard variation of the signal were evaluated. For the right camera, the calculated value was

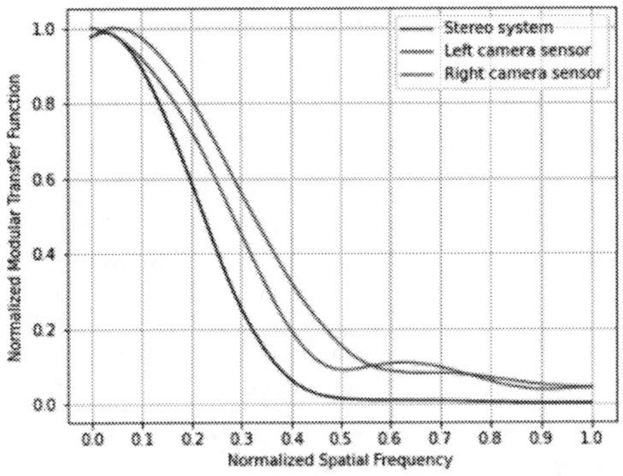

Figure 7. MTF of each camera sensor and combined system.

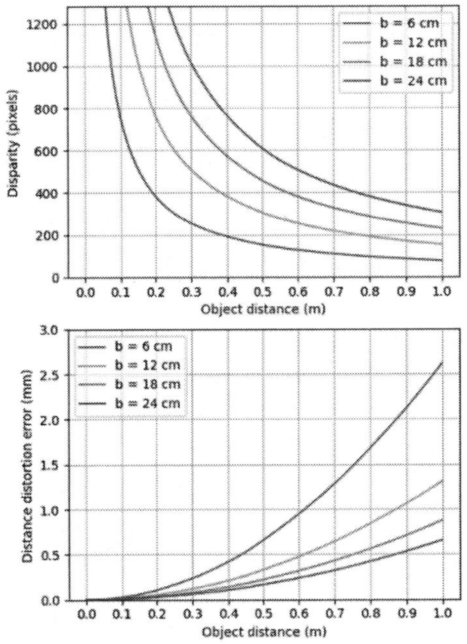

Figure 8. Baseline distance disparity and distortion error evaluation.

19.7 dB, while for the left camera it was 17.9 dB, below the 36 dB specified by the manufacturer.

D. Stereo vision parameters

The first step in tuning the stereo system is to define the baseline distance that will be used to capture the images. The developed prototype has a minimum possible baseline of 6 cm and a maximum of 24 cm, which makes it capable of simulating human vision, which has this value in the range of 5.4 to 7.4 cm, in addition to allowing the exploration of other scenarios. For this, considering (3) and (4), the expected disparity for an object up to 1 m away from the camera and the expected distortion error at such distance were calculated, for four values of baseline, 6 cm, 12 cm, 18 cm and 24 cm, as can be seen in the Figure 8, considering the resolution of 1280 x 960.

When setting the baseline distance, it is always preferable to use the lower values to ensure greater interpolation between the two generated images, which allows closer objects to have their distance calculated. For example, according to the graph shown, for b = 24 cm, objects up to 23.8 cm away from the camera would not be present in both images, making it impossible to calculate the disparity, while for b = 6 cm such a situation is only valid for objects less than 5.9 cm away. As for objects of up to 1 m, the distortion error proved to be small for all cases, including for the scenario with the smallest baseline, so it can be defined that the best use of the stereo system occurs for values close to 6 cm.

Thus, for b = 6 cm and height of 1 m (value chosen so that, due to the height of the growing plants, the object under analysis is not too close to the sensors), the calibrated parameters results of the left and right cameras, and of the stereo system, were:

$$\textit{Left camera matrix} = \begin{bmatrix} 736 & 0 & 582 \\ 0 & 735 & 464 \\ 0 & 0 & 1 \end{bmatrix} \tag{8}$$

$$\textit{Left distortion coefficients} = \begin{bmatrix} 0.0589 \\ -0.169 \\ 0.00139 \\ 0.00198 \\ 0.142 \end{bmatrix}^{\mathrm{T}} \tag{9}$$

$$\textit{Right camera matrix} = \begin{bmatrix} 1480 & 0 & 681 \\ 0 & 1480 & 480 \\ 0 & 0 & 1 \end{bmatrix} \tag{10}$$

$$\textit{Right distortion coefficients} = \begin{bmatrix} -0.0728 \\ 3.98 \\ 0.00117 \\ 0.00630 \\ -22.6 \end{bmatrix}^{\mathrm{T}} \tag{11}$$

$$\mathbf{R_x} = \begin{bmatrix} 0.960 & -0.0133 & -0.281 \\ 0.0159 & 1.00 & 0.00721 \\ 0.280 & -0.0114 & 0.960 \end{bmatrix} \tag{12}$$

$$\mathbf{T_x} = \begin{bmatrix} -0.787 \\ -0.0670 \\ 5.65 \end{bmatrix} \tag{13}$$

Note that if the baseline distance is changed, it is necessary to calibrate the system again, recalculating only the $\mathbf{R_x}$ and $\mathbf{T_x}$ matrices, but it is expected that $\mathbf{R_x}$ will not change significantly, as the mounted structure does not allow the cameras to yaw, pitch or roll.

IV. Conclusion and Future Work

The results showed a characterization process of an IoT stereo image sensor system, capable of capturing and transferring validated images via wireless commands, ready to be used in real agricultural field conditions. Such developed embedded vision system can be useful for applications in 3D image processing, with several variable parameters that allow the adaptation of the system to different situations, although the power supply can be simplified to reduce the weight and power spent of the system, allowing the use of smaller batteries and fewer components (for example, with only a 12 Vdc to 5 Vdc converter and 9 W 12 V LED lamp).

For future steps, it is desired to carry out agricultural analyzes, considering weed families, as well as the inclusion of AI-based weed image process to identify plant species for agricultural control. In addition, an expansion of system's connectivity with other devices will also be realized.

Acknowledgment

This work has been supported by Embrapa and Brazilian research agency CAPES.

References

[1] FAO, "The future of food and agriculture – alternative pathways to 2050," Food and Agriculture Organization of the United Nations Rome, pp. 224, 2018.

[2] H. Abouziena and W. Haggag, "Weed control in clean agriculture: a review," Planta daninha, SciELO Brasil, vol. 34, pp. 377–-392, 2016.

[3] S. C. Bhatla and M. A. Lal, "Plant physiology, development and metabolism," Springer, 2018.

[4] B. M. Moreno and P. E. Cruvinel, "Sensors-based stereo image system for precision control of weed in the agricultural industry," SENSORDEVICES 2018, The Ninth International Conference on Sensor Device Technologies and Applications, pp. 69–76, 2018.

[5] B. M. Moreno and P. E. Cruvinel, "Computer vision system for identifying on farming weed species," 2022 IEEE 16th International Conference on Semantic Computing (ICSC), USA, pp. 287–292, 2022.

[6] M. I. Sadiq, S. M. P. Rahman, S. Kayes, A. H. Sumaita, and N. A. Chisty, "A review on the imaging approaches in agriculture with crop and soil sensing methodologies," 2021 Fifth International Conference On Intelligent Computing in Data Sciences (ICDS), Morocco, pp. 1–7, 2021.

[7] M. Rajoriya and T. Usha, "Pattern recognition in agricultural areas," Journal of Critical Reviews, vol. 7, pp. 1123–1127, 2020.

[8] J. Wäldchen, M. Rzanny, M. Seeland, and P. Mäder, "Automated plant species identification—trends and future directions," PLoS computational biology, vol. 14, pp. 1–19, 2018.

[9] M. P. Raj, P. R. Swaminarayan, J. R. Saini, and D. K. Parmar, "Applications of pattern recognition algorithms in agriculture: a review," International Journal of Advanced Networking and Applications, vol. 6, pp. 2495–2502, 2015.

[10] D. Mcloughlin, "Image processing apparatus for analysis of vegetation for weed control by identifying types of weeds," EP1000540, May 17, 2000.

[11] J. Gao and Z. Jin, "Bionic four-foot walking intelligent rotary tillage weeding device, has weeding system installed on back side of machine body, where gear in gear rotating mechanism transmits power to rotary shaft that is provided with weeding cutter," CN114794067, Jul 29, 2022.

[12] X. Jin, Y. Chen, and J. Yu, "Precise weeding method for lawn and pasture based on cloud-killing spectrum, involves receiving images uploaded by each weeding robot, completing weed identification and outputting spraying instructions, and collecting and organizing massive weed data for big data applications," CN113349188, Sep 7, 2021.

[13] S. E. Mathe, M. Bandaru, H. K. Kondaveeti, S. Vappangi, and G. S. Rao, "A survey of agriculture applications utilizing raspberry pi," 2022 International Conference on Innovative Trends in Information Technology (ICITIIT), Kottayam, India, pp. 1–7, 2022.

[14] C. Balamurugan and R. Satheesh, "Development of raspberry pi and IoT based monitoring and controlling devices for agriculture," pp. 207–215, 2017.

[15] K. A. Patil and N. R. Kale, "A model for smart agriculture using IoT," 2016 International Conference on Global Trends in Signal Processing, Information Computing and Communication (ICGTSPICC), Jalgaon, India, pp. 543–545, 2016.

[16] O. van Zwanenberg, S. Triantaphillidou, R. Jenkin, and A. Psarrou, "Edge detection techniques for quantifying spatial imaging system performance and image quality," in Proceedings of the IEEE/CVF Conference on Computer Vision and Pattern Recognition Workshops, pp. 1871–1879, 2019.

[17] N. Kawagishi, R. Kakinuma, and H. Yamamoto, "Aerial image resolution measurement based on the slanted knife edge method," in Optics Express Vol. 28, pp. 35518–35527, 2020.

[18] A. A. Naumov, A. V. Gorevoy, A. S. Machikhin, V. I. Batshev, and V. E. Pozha, "Estimating the quality of stereoscopic endoscopic systems," in Journal of Physics: Conference Series Vol. 1421, pp. 012044, 2019.

[19] L. Yang, B. Wang, R. Zhang, H. Zhou, and R. Wang, "Analysis on location accuracy for the binocular stereo vision system," in IEEE Photonics Journal, vol. 10, no. 1, pp. 1–16, Art no. 7800316, Feb. 2018.

[20] Y. M. Wang, Y. Li, and J. B. Zheng, "A camera calibration technique based on OpenCV," The 3rd International Conference on Information Sciences and Interaction Sciences, Chengdu, China, pp. 403–406, 2010.

[21] J. Sun, X. Chen, Z. Gong, Z. Liu, and Y. Zhao, "Accurate camera calibration with distortion models using sphere images," in Optics & Laser Technology, Vol. 65, pp. 83–87, 2015.

[22] J. Salvi, X. Armangué, and J. Batlle, "A comparative review of camera calibrating methods with accuracy evaluation," in Pattern Recognition, Vol.35, Issue 7, pp. 1617–1635, 2002.

[23] S. Yang, Y. Gao, Z. Liu, and G. Zhang, "A calibration method for binocular stereo vision sensor with short-baseline based on 3D flexible control field," in Optics and Lasers in Engineering, Vol. 124, pp. 105817, 2020.

[24] Y. Wang, X. Wang, Z. Wan, and J. Zhang, "A method for extrinsic parameter calibration of rotating binocular stereo vision using a single feature point," in Sensors, Vol. 18, Art no. 3666, pp. 1–16, 2018.

Developing Affordable Sensors in Agriculture Based on Results Obtained at Embrapa Instrumentation

Paulo S. de P. Herrmann[1], Ladislau M. Rabello[1], Victor Bertucci Neto[1], Paulo E. Cruvinel[1,2]

[1] Embrapa Instrumentation (CNPDIA), [2] Computer Science Program, Federal University of Sao Carlos
Sao Carlos, SP, Brazil. e-mail; paulo.herrmann@embrapa.br ladislau.rabello@embrapa.br victor.bertucci@embrapa.br
paulo.cruvinel@embrapa.br

Abstract— **Agricultural sensors are crucial in improving crop yields and reducing resource waste. It has led researchers to develop affordable sensors that can be easily integrated into existing farming systems. Developing inexpensive sensors involves using low-cost materials and simple manufacturing methods, ensuring reliable and accurate measurements. One of Embrapa Instrumentation's objectives is the research and development of sensors applied to agriculture. This article briefly discusses a sensor for soil moisture measurement using the microwave technique; a system for measuring the apparent electrical conductivity of soils; a Sensor for measuring water and plant relationships; and the Sensor for evaluating spray solution concentration to control weeds to improve crop yield and reduce water. Using affordable sensors in agriculture can provide an effective and sustainable solution to enhance the productivity of small and medium farms, thus increasing food security and supporting sustainable agriculture.**

Keywords** - **Affordable sensors; Agriculture; soil moisture; soil resistance; water-plant measuring; spray quality; pest control.

I. INTRODUCTION

The applications of sensors in general, and more specifically, affordable sensors, are the basis for developing devices for instrumentation, automation, precision agriculture, and digital agriculture.

The global agricultural sensors market size was valued at USD 4.74 billion in 2021. It is expected to reach USD 16.83 billion by 2030, growing at a Compound annual growth rate (CAGR) of 15.12% during the forecast period (2022–2030) [1].

The low-cost sensor is a technology initially developed for consumer and research applications. Competitive and low-cost due to economies of scale, these sensor technologies allow new applications or more economical use of sensors in production and environments [2].

Despite being used in research, most field sensors are still in their infancy in their commercial relationship. Soil moisture sensors can be mentioned, sensors that can correlate fertility, scales that could indicate performance, sensors, and indicators of pests and diseases, among others, and if they were present in the field, they could be connected to IoT (Internet of things) [3]–[5].

Below is a brief discussion of affordable sensors for agriculture, which were developed at Embrapa Instrumentation. In the next sections there are the descriptions of the recent development of affordable sensors, which are: a sensor for measuring soil moisture using microwaves with two techniques (waveguide and free space); a system for measuring the apparent electrical conductivity of ECa soils; a sensor for measuring the water and plant relationship; and a sensor to evaluate spray solution concentration to control weeds to improve crop yield and reduce water.

The sensors listed have something in common: they are affordable and designed to be used in agricultural environments. They are capable of measuring different aspects of the environment, such as soil, water, plants, and weed control. Additionally, they can be integrated into IoT technologies.

II. SENSOR FOR SOIL MOISTURE MEASUREMENT, USING MICROWAVE TECHNIQUES

The content and availability of water in the soil are parameters of fundamental importance in the various fields of basic and applied science, as well as in technologies for agriculture, geology, meteorology, hydrology, and various areas of engineering.

The most used techniques for measuring soil water are gravimetric, neutron moderation and gamma-ray attenuation, Time Domain Reflectometry (TDR), and remote sensing.

Through the interaction of electromagnetic waves, at microwave frequency, with the water-soil system, greater or lesser attenuation of the signal is obtained depending on the volumetric moisture content present. Figure 1 presents a system for measuring soil moisture content that uses microwave signal transmission and reception through the waveguide technique, in the X band, with an operating frequency of 10 GHz and a power of 25 mW. In tests carried out at the laboratory level, we proved the correlation of the attenuation in dB with the volumetric humidity in clayey, sandy, and glass microsphere soils [6].

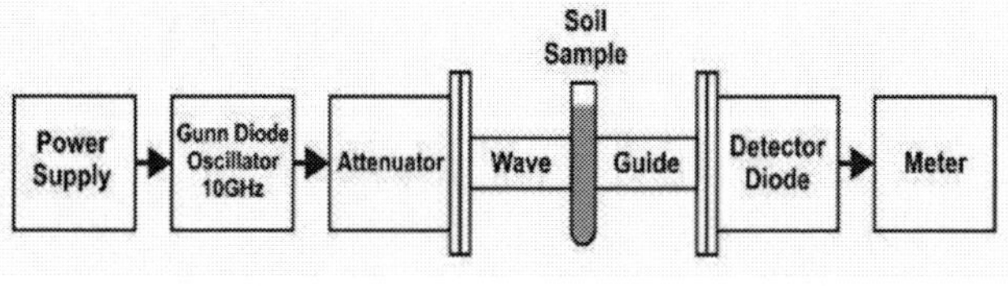

Figure 1. Presents a system for measuring soil moisture content that uses microwave signal transmission and reception through the waveguide technique.

Figure 2 presents the results that show the influence of water in the water-soil system, in the attenuation of microwaves, through the relation of the attenuation of the signal in dB by the volumetric soil moisture in sandy soil (1.20 < soil density (g/cm^3) < 1.26), clayey (0.83 < soil density (g/cm^3) < 0.92)) and glass microsphere (1.13 < soil density (g/cm3) < 1.19)). The error in sample preparation was 4.7%. All measurements were conducted under laboratory conditions (room temperature ~23.0 ± 0.5 0C and relative humidity 36%).

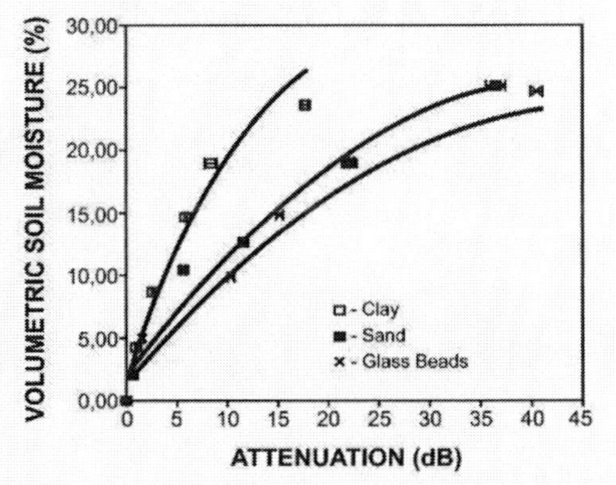

Figure 2. The attenuation calibration curve in dB, as a function of the volumetric soil moisture of the samples

A network analyzer, model 8510 from Hewlett-Packard, was used, evaluating the parameter insertion loss S_{21} (dB) to compare with the results obtained in the attenuation system in dB. Figure 3 presents the results for all samples with a linear regression where their r^2 was 0.976.

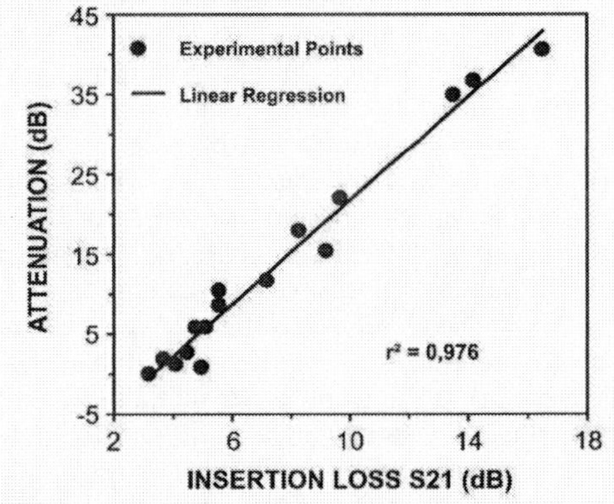

Figure 3. Comparison between the results obtained with the proposed system and those obtained the insertion loss S_{21} (dB), using the 8510 HP network analyzer.

Investigating the behavior of plant root system growth as a function of soil water is essential for studying root physiology. Figure 4 shows a non-invasive tool based on the transmittance of electromagnetic waves in the microwave frequency range, operating close to 4.8 GHz, which was developed using microstrip patch antennas to determine volumetric soil moisture in rhizoboxes. Antennas were placed on both sides of the rhizobox, and the S parameters were measured using a vector network analyzer.

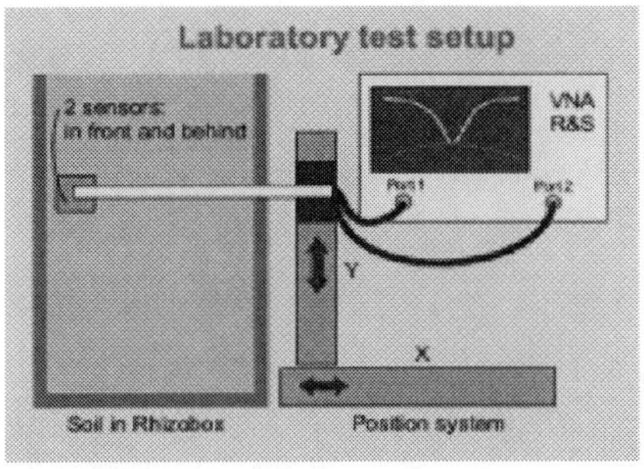

Figure 4. Block diagram of the system developed to measure S21 (dB) of soil moisture in the rhizobox, using the Vector Network Analyzer, in the microwave frequency range (4.6–5.0 GHz).

The dispersion parameter S_{21}(dB) was also used to show the effect of different soil types and temperatures on the measurement. In addition, the sensitivity, reproducibility, and repeatability of the system were evaluated (Figure 5). The measurement was carried out three times to each dot (n = 3). The red dots represent the reproducibility (98.9%) averages, and the black dots represent the repeatability (93.0%) averages. The quantitative results of soil moisture, measured in rhizoboxes, presented in this work, demonstrate that the microwave technique using microstrip patch antennas is a reliable non-invasive, and accurate system, and has shown potentially promising applications for measurement of roots based on rhizobox phenotyping [7].

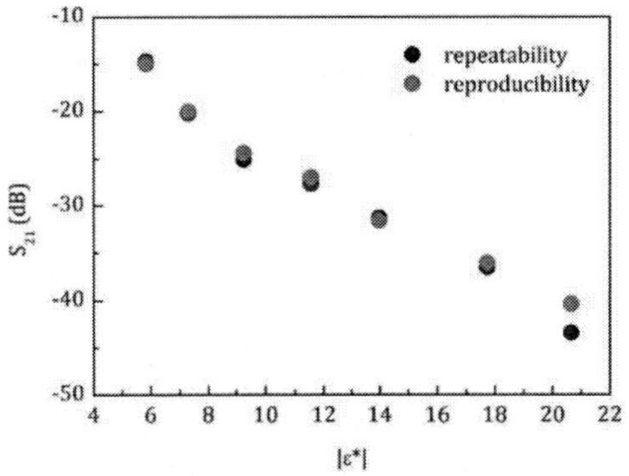

Figure 5. The relation between $|\varepsilon^*|$ versus the average of S_{21} (dB) shows the repeatability and reproducibility of the system developed were calculated.

Figure 6 shows the relationship between the S_{21} measured with the developed system and the volumetric soil moisture θ_V (%) determined and calculated by the second and third-order polynomial equation. The calibration was obtained using four (04) samples, which are: Cerrado Soil (squares), Kaktus Soil (open circles), and Glass Beads (triangles). The experiment was carried out at the standard laboratory ambient conditions (Temperature (T(°C)) = 25.0 ± 0.5 °C and Relative Humidity (RH(%)) 30%).

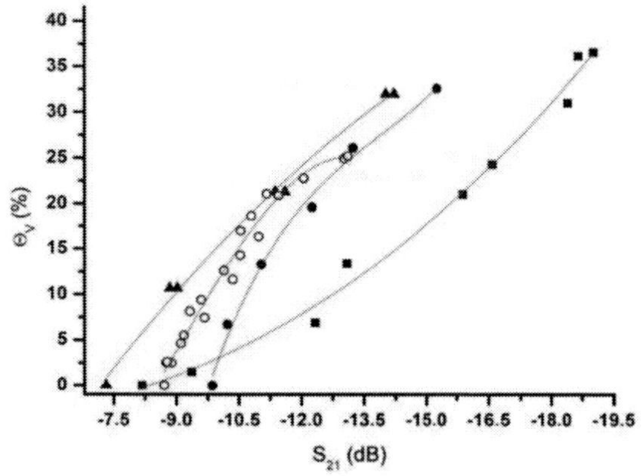

Figure 6. Relationship between the S_{21} measured with the developed system and the volumetric soil moisture θ_V (%). The four (04) samples used are Cerrado Soil (squares), Kaktus Soil (open circles) and Glass Beads (triangles).

III. SYSTEM FOR MEASURING THE APPARENT ELECTRICAL CONDUCTIVITY OF SOILS ECa

Soil apparent electrical conductivity (ECa) originated from measuring soil salinity, a pertinent problem in arid zones associated with irrigated crops and areas with shallow water tables. Soil ECa is greatly influenced by a vast combination of physical and chemical properties of the soil, such as soluble salts; mineralogy and clay content; the amount of water present in the soil; volumetric density; organic matter, and soil temperature.

The most effective application of apparent soil electrical conductivity is at field scale in mapping the spatial variability of many edaphic properties, e.g., organic matter, moisture, and in the determination of a wide variety of anthropogenic properties, such as: leaching fraction; irrigation and drainage patterns; compaction patterns due to machinery [8].

Soil ECa is a quick, more reliable, and easy tool than other techniques, but it only sometimes correlates with crop yield. Therefore, the ECa measurement is among the most frequent tools used in research in precision agriculture for the space-time characterization of edaphic and anthropogenic properties that influence crop productivity.

The measurement of electrical conductivity (σ) originates from the measurement of electrical resistivity (ρ), which consists of using a sample of known shapes and dimensions (square, cylindrical, and others).

The electrical resistance is then calculated by the following equation:

$$R = \rho\left(\frac{L}{A}\right) \qquad (1)$$

Where:

R = electrical resistance [Ohms, Ω];
ρ = electrical resistivity [Ohms x centimeters, Ω.cm];
L = sample length [cm, cm].

For samples of undefined shapes and dimensions, the method known as the four-point system [9] [10] is used, Figure 7, which consists of using four metal electrodes sequentially aligned with known distances.

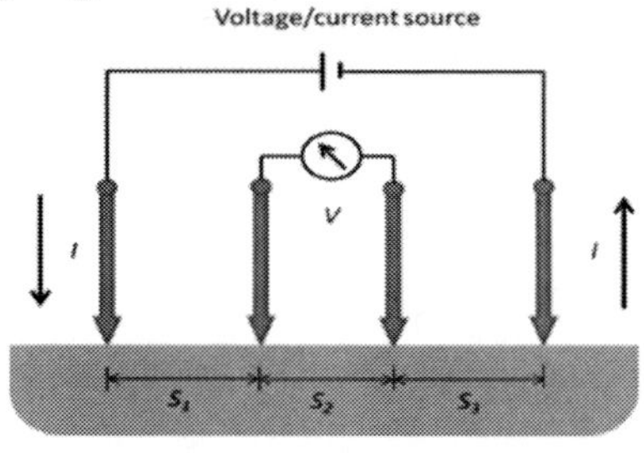

Figure 7. Four-point system.

Applying electrical current I (Ampere) to the outer electrodes and with a voltage V (Volts) reading from the two center electrodes. The resistivity is then calculated with the following equation:

$$\rho = \frac{2.\pi\left(\frac{V}{I}\right)}{\frac{1}{S_1} + \frac{1}{S_2} - \frac{1}{S_1 + S_2} - \frac{1}{S_2 + S_3}} \qquad (2)$$

Electrical conductivity, σ, is defined as the inverse of electrical resistivity, so we have:

$$\sigma = \frac{1}{\rho} \qquad (3)$$

Figure 8 illustrates the block diagram of the developed system, which uses the PIC18F258 manufactured by Microchip Technology [20] as its central processor. The system was designed for reading two four-point measurement systems, consisting of two voltmeters, one of unitary gain and the other of gain three for deeper measurements, an alternating voltage source of 159 Hz for measuring electric current, three signal filters for reading channels, three alternating to continuous signal converters, 1024 bits; 1 bit resolution; 4.88×10^{-3} Volts dc; 32-character LCD (Liquid Crystal Display) for viewing electrical conductivity measurements and control information, four-function keyboard for user-machine communication; standard RS232 serial port for communication and transfer of stored data and NMEA (National Marine Electronics Association) sentences for GNSS (Global Navigation Satellite System) system and flash memory for storage of collected data, the capacity of 64 KBytes, in Figure 9 the system is illustrated.

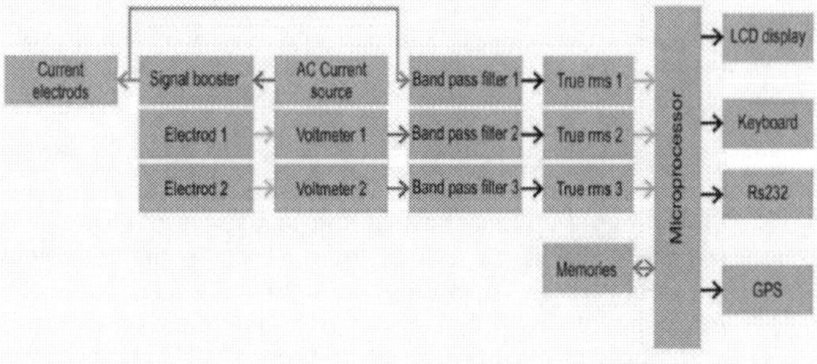

Figure 8. Apparent electrical conductivity system block diagram.

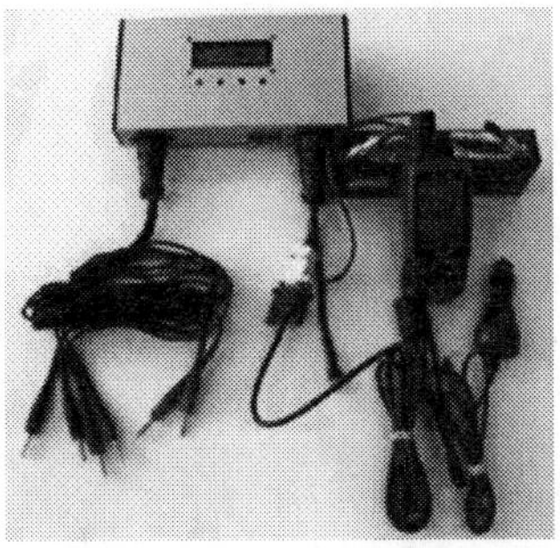

Figure 9. Electrical conductivity measurement system.

Figure 10 illustrates measurements taken using the system in an area where vines are planted in the study and definition of homogeneous areas for this crop.

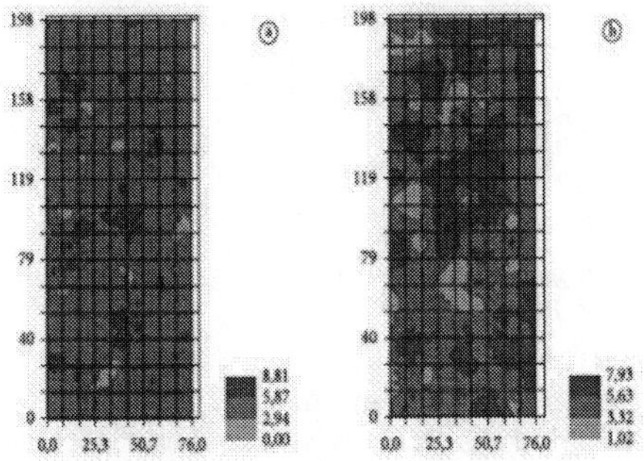

Figure 10. Maps of homogeneous zones of apparent soil electrical conductivity, a - ECa at a depth of 0.3 m; b - ECa at depth 0.9 m, grapevine crop, semi-arid region, Brazil

Continuing the work with a conductivity measurement system, we evaluated the possibilities of implementing direct reading of soil electrical conductivity data and making them available in the cloud for analysis in artificial intelligence, making these data available to interested parties, direct integration with productivity maps, soil attributes, soil fertility for decision-making in crop management possibly in real time, configurations for variable rate application systems, updating of the technology used due to the constant modernization of these technologies, making it possible to expand the system for the use of IoT and use of programming for cell phones .

IV. SENSOR FOR MEASURING WATER AND PLANT RELATIONSHIPS

Studies in water relations of higher plants often present many ongoing debates about the mechanisms responsible for the ascent of water in plants. In the 70's, one of the most useful techniques to aid in direct measurements of plant cells, called the pressure probe [11], was developed. It consisted of a glass capillary connected to a chamber filled with oil that punctured the cell wall, thus establishing a hydraulic connection between the cell sap and oil content.

Using an optical microscope, it was possible to measure the movement of the oil/cell sap boundary, the meniscus, and then by raising or lowering the oil pressure inside the chamber mechanically until the meniscus returned to its original position, one could measure the pressure with a sensor in the oil chamber. Through this technique, as well as a series of improvements (such as system automation), it was possible to more accurately determine how plant cell pressure varies under different physical conditions, thus enabling an understanding of the hydraulic conductivity of cell membranes and the volumetric modulus of the cell's elasticity [12].

Unfortunately, there had not been a detailed physical model describing how to calculate measurement errors, time constants, dynamical behavior, and temperature correlation. Bertucci Neto [13] developed a physical model of the pressure probe and proposed an automated pressure probe based on thermal, instead of mechanical, compensation [13].

The meniscus movement could be parameterized and correlated with the pressure applied to the capillary tip. One of the detection techniques developed was based on video image digitization. A single video line related to the meniscus position was striped and digitized. In this manner, the meniscus position is correlated to the time base. In Figure 11 the whole video image is shown, while Figure 12 shows the information of a video frame and a striped video line related to the meniscus position.

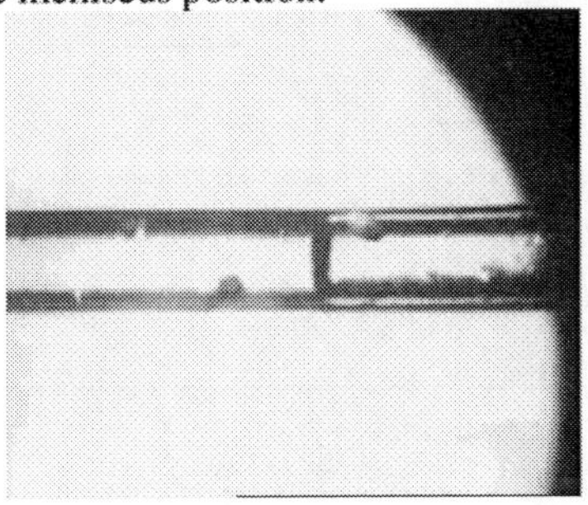

Figure 11. Video image of the meniscus in the capillary.

The information obtained on the single video line is shown in Figure 13 as well as the digitized signal. The other technique was based on image treatment (through LabView). The meniscus positional datum was used to control the system and return the meniscus to its original position through a feedback loop. Through the camera signal, it was, therefore, possible to select a region in the image in which a single video line carried the entirety of the data on the meniscus' position. As predicted in the modeling study, the relationship between electric heating voltage and the meniscus position in pixels is quadratic, as shown in Figure 14. The quadratic approximation presents a standard deviation of less than 10 pixels. By using a feedback loop and including a PID controller, it was possible to keep the meniscus in its original position after a pressure step input.

This is shown in Figure 14, where the measured and modeling responses are compared. Although dynamical measurements can present large errors, primarily during short meniscus movements, the techniques can be appropriated to measure long-term pressure variations in plant cells.

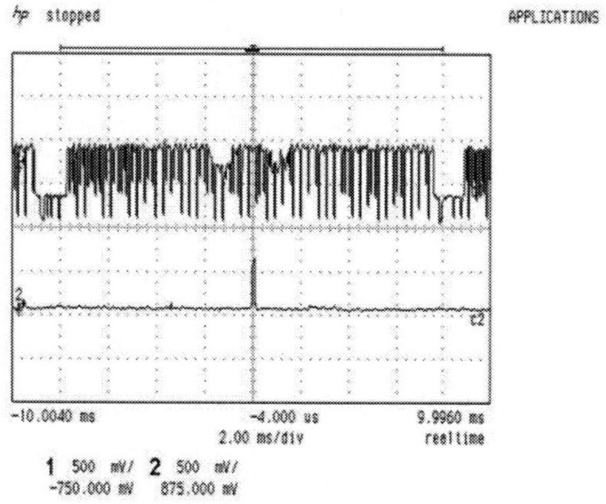

Figure 12. Oscilloscope signal. Above: Video signal of 262.5 lines of a frame. Down: Single video line stripped from the frame in the region of the meniscus image.

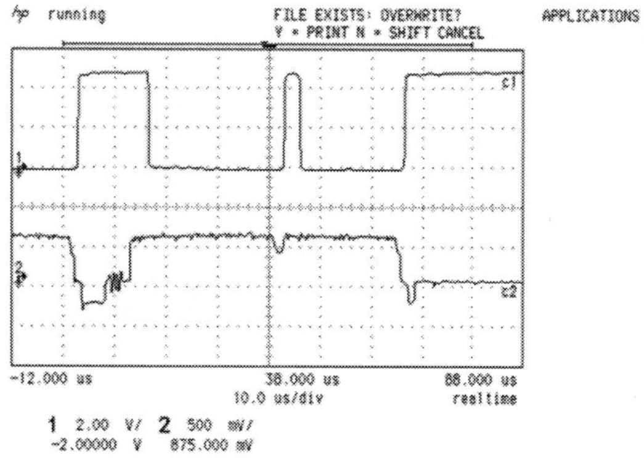

Figure 13. Oscilloscope signal. Above: digitized signal after the voltage comparator. Down: voltage information of the single video line.

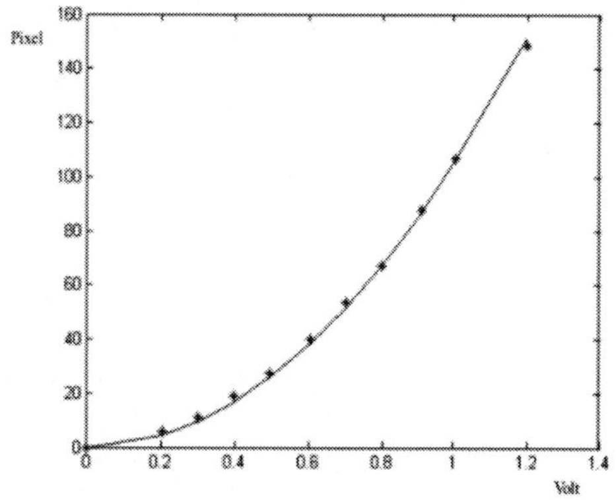

Figure 14. Quadratic behavior between electric power in volt and meniscus' displacement.

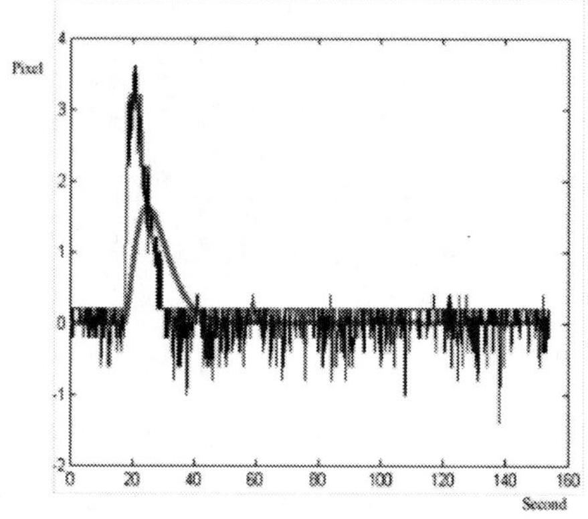

Figure 15. Meniscus returning to the origin position after a pressure step at the tip of the capillary due to the PID control action. Red line: simulated response; black line: measured response.

V. SENSOR FOR THE PH REAL TIME MEASUREMENTS IN AGRICULTURAL SPRAY SOLUTION

The pH is a scale from 0 to 14 used to determine the degree of acidity of a solution, being possible to classify it as acidic (pH < 7), basic (pH > 7), or neutral (pH = 7). It is based on the degree of acidity of an aqueous solution based on the concentration of hydronium ions (H3O+).

Acidic solutions have excess hydronium ions and a pH lower than 7. On the other hand, basic solutions have an excess of hydroxyl ions (OH-) and pH values greater than 7. In addition, solutions considered neutral have the same concentration of H_3O+ ions and OH- ions, and their pH measurement is 7.

The negative logarithm of the molar concentration of H3O+ ions in the form can obtain the pH measurement:

$$pH = -\log[H_3O^+] \qquad (4)$$

Naturally when one is considering water the process of auto-ionization has the same amount of H_3O+ and OH- ions. Therefore, aqueous solutions of any substance have these two types of ions, and the condition of acidity or basicity of the medium is defined by the ratio between the amounts of H_3O+ and OH-, so as follows (Table I).

TABLE I. MEDIUM AND STATUS IN TERMS OF THE PH OCCURRENCE.

medium	status
Acid	excess H_3O^+ ions
Basic	excess OH^- ions
Neutral	equal amounts of H_3O^+ and OH^- ions

Hydronium ions are formally represented as H_3O+. However, it is common to find the notation H+ for hydronium ions or to refer to the acidity of a medium.

Pesticides, insecticides, and herbicides have their effectiveness modified by the pH of the solution resulting from the preparation of syrup that involves the active agent of these products and water.

Generally, for weed control, herbicides are used, which work better in slightly acidic pH, around pH 4 to 6, and in some exceptions may act better in slightly alkaline. Glyphosate, for example, acts preferentially between pH 3.5 to 5.0, being a weak acid [14] [15].

At this pH of the spray solution, the ions are dissociated, favoring the foliar absorption of glyphosate due to the greater ease of crossing cell membranes, increasing the effectiveness of the product [16]. Besides, the effectiveness of glyphosate is affected both by the pH of the medium and by the presence of cations in the spray water [17].

The above or below ideal range can initiate degradation of the molecule, or hydrolysis. For example, when a weak acidic herbicide is mixed in a solution with an acidic pH, it tends to remain intact, however if it is mixed in a solution with an alkaline pH, it can result in the breakdown of molecules. In fact, despite many pesticides having a buffering effect in their formulations, special attention should be considered in pH value monitoring. Therefore, regardless of the pH of the pre-existing spray solution, one may adjust to the pH close to the ideal of each formulation.

This is a fact that the producer must be aware of, especially in mixtures with fungicides and insecticides, which may have negative effects on the effectiveness of other pesticides.

A pH sensor has been developed to operate in real time directly embedded into a spray nozzle, which is located on the spray boom (Figure 16).

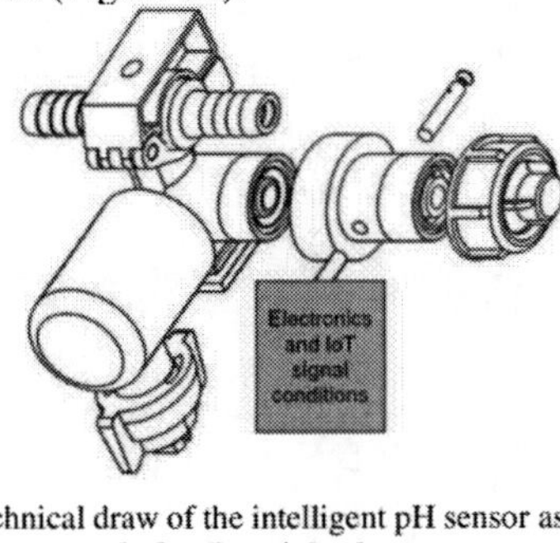

Figure 16. Technical draw of the intelligent pH sensor assembled on the nozzle for direct injection sprayer.

It has been used as a Raspberry Pi (RPi) due to its powerful processor, rich I/O interface and Internet of Things (IoT) capability, which allowed the remote control across existing spray boom infrastructure and reduced human intervention [18]. Besides, the developed IoT pH system can gather measurements data for intelligent evaluation by resident software.

The RPi is a mini-embedded computer developed in the United Kingdom by the Raspberry Pi Foundation in association with Broadcom. The model used was the RPi 3 B+, where its specifications can be seen in Table II.

TABLE II. RASPBERRY PI 3 MODEL B+ CHARACTERISTICS

Processor	BCM2837B0 Cortex-A53 (ARMv8) 64-bit		
Clock	1.4 GHz	GPIO	40 pins
Memory	1 GB SDRAM	Gigabit Ethernet	1 connector
USB Port	4 USB 2.0	HDMI	1 connector
Camera serial interface (CSI)		Display serial interface (DSI)	
Wireless (dual band)		Bluetooth 4.2/BLE	
3,5mm 4 Jack output		Micro SD card slot	
Support Power-over-Ethernet		Input DC 5V/2.5A	

The internal memory is defined using a micro SD card, where the kernel of the operating system is also present, being recommended the use of at least 8 GB of memory. In addition, the RPi 3 B+, unlike previous family models, enables BCM43438 wireless LAN and Bluetooth Low Energy (BLE) communication, allowing wireless data exchange.

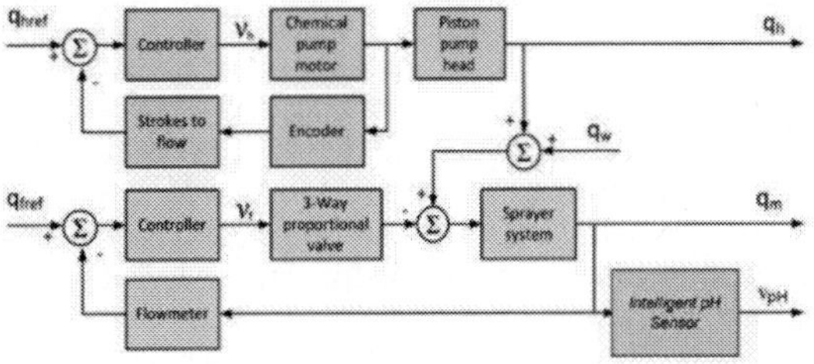

Figure 17. Block diagram for the fungicides, herbicides or insecticides, mixture control, and the intelligent pH sensor.

When it is being applied to a direct injection sprayer it has a typical control loop as shown in Figure 17. In this figure, the upper blocks indicate the direct injection components and corresponding variables q_{href}, V_h, and q_h, which represent the set point for the chemical flow, controlled, and measured variables respectively. In the lower blocks, at the same figure, is possible to observe the sprayer components, which are described as qfref, Vf, and qm, which represent the set point for the mixture flow, controlled, and measured variables respectively. In this type of direct injection sprayer, the injection point is located upstream from the sprayer pump as presented in [18], and [19]. The water flow qw is dependent on both the flow mixture qm and the injection flow qh. The intelligent sensor is assembled to measure the pH of the spray solution, which is proportional to its output denoted VpH.

Figure 18 shows the flow-diagram of the algorithm for real time self-diagnostics.

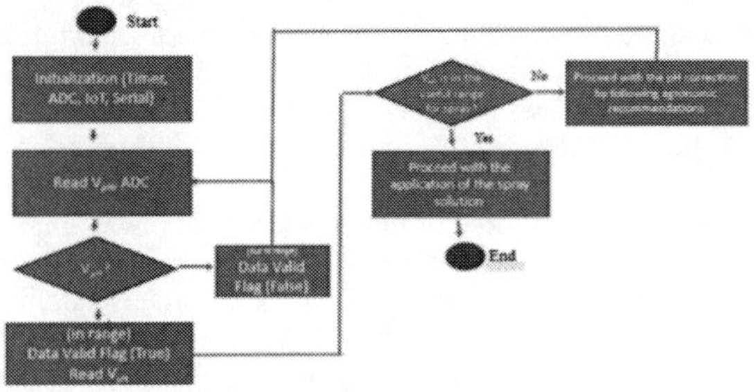

Figure 18. Computational Flow diagram for the real time measurements and flag related to the spray solution pH evaluation.

The calibration curve for the intelligent sensor for pH measurements is presented in Figure 19

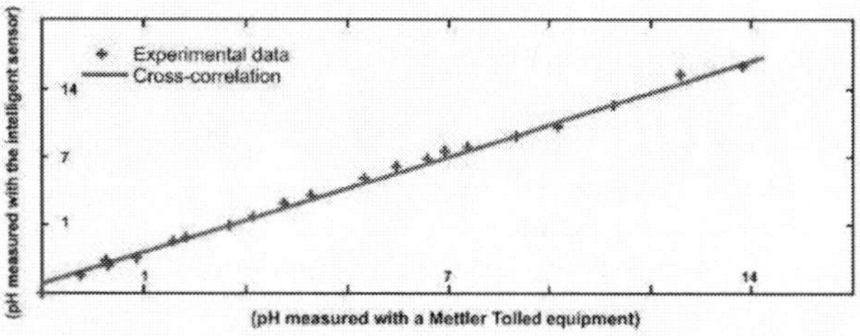

Figure 19. Calibration Curve and comparison with values obtained with prepared solutions with well-known pH values.

Using the microwave techniques since the temperature affects the error of volumetric soil moisture measurements; a calibration curve requires information on soil temperature and soil water content. The distinct effect of porous media on the calibration curve (S_{21} (dB) vs θ_V (%)) was also observed, giving the opportunity to use such an approach to investigate plant root growth in different soil types and moisture.

Techniques that allow deepening the study of water relations in plants are impacting areas of Agronomic Engineering in addition to cutting-edge areas such as Plant Phenotyping.

The information provided by the intelligent pH sensor could be in the form of a flag, which shows a confidence level of the spray solution quality during its applications. Furthermore, the results show additional information than traditional sensors and meet prospects in practical applications, bringing potential benefits for sustainability, precision agriculture processes, and the potential to be used in IoT systems. His configurations will depend on demand and large-scale applications.

VI. CONCLUSIONS

Using the sensor developed with microwave technique (waveguide and microstrip antenna) in the GHz frequency, is possible to see that the main benefits with the instrument proposed here, that are: the use of a non-destructive methodology, easy measurement of soil water, portability, the use of non-ionizing radiation, speed in the measurement and low cost.

The use of the apparent electrical conductivity of the soil has demonstrated as an important tool for precision agricultural work, its ease, simplicity and practicality lead to time and cost savings in carrying out decision-making in the areas of management and spatial variability of study areas. But ECa alone does not answer all questions needed after the data mosaic she provides, mine that data and make it more user friendly.

The physical model of the pressure probe was improved, and an automated pressure gauge was developed to investigate the displacement of the meniscus in the observation of the water-plant ratio.

An intelligent sensor to measure the pH of spray systems based on direct injection was presented. The results have shown its usability in real time applications. The decision to embed such an intelligent sensor directly in the sprayer nozzle provides a scenario that can be useful to avoid losses in agricultural production.

ACKNOWLEDGMENT

This work has been supported by the following Brazilian research agencies: Embrapa Instrumentation and Embrapa Labex – Europe

REFERENCES

[1] Agricultural Sensors Market Growth, Share, Forecast to 2030. https://straitsresearch.com/report/agricutural-sensors-market#:~:text=Market%20Snapshot&text=The%20global%20agricultural%20sensors%20market,period%20(2022%E2%80%932030). 2021 (accessed in 15/02/2023).

[2] M. Kückelhaus, and G. Chung, "Logistics Trend Radar, DHL Customer Solutions & Innovation", Germany. Retrieved from www.dhl.com. 2013 (Accessed 03.07.2018).

[3] T. M. Banhazi, et al. "Precision livestock farming: An international review of scientific and commercial aspects." International Journal of Agricultural and Biological Engineering, v.5, Iss.: 3, pp. 1-9, 2012.

[4] P. E. Cruvinel and L. Martin Neto, "Subsídios para o desenvolvimento do agronegócio brasileiro: o programa automação agropecuária, visão e estratégias. (Subsidies for the development of Brazilian agribusiness: the agricultural automation program, vision and strategies.)" Comunicado Técnico, Embrapa Instrumentação, n. 32, set/99, p. 1-4, 1999.

[5] G. S. Hundal, C. M. Laux, D. Buckmaster, M. J. Sutton, and M. Langemeier, "Exploring Barriers to the Adoption of Internet of Things-Based Precision Agriculture Practices." Agriculture, 13, 163, 2023, https://doi.org/10.3390/agriculture13010163.

[6] P. S. P. Herrmann. "Caracterização de um equipamento para medida de umidade do solo através de técnica de microondas." (Characterization of an equipment for measuring soil moisture using the microwave technique.). Eng. M.Sc Dissertation. Escola de Engenharia de São Carlos, Departamento de Engenharia Elétrica. 1993.

[7] P. S. P. Herrmann, V. Sydoruk, and F. N. Marques Porto, "Microwave Transmittance Technique Using Microstrip Patch Antennas, as a Non-Invasive Tool to Determine Soil Moisture in Rhizoboxes". Sensors, v. 20, p. 1166, 2020.

[8] D. R. Nielsen, J. W. Biggar, and K. T. Erh, "Spatial variability of field-measurement soil-water properties." Hilgardia, Berkeley, v. 42, n. 7, p. 215-259, 1973

[9] F. M. Smits, "Measurement of sheet resistivities with the four-point probe", Bell System Technical Journal, New York, p. 711-718, May 1958.

[10] W. R. Runyan, "Semiconductor measurement and instrumentation." New York: McGraw-Hill book, c1975, Cap. 3.

[11] D. Hüsken, E. Steudle, and U. Zimmermann, "Pressure probe technique for measuring water relations of cells in higher plants." Plant Physiology. v. 61. p. 158-163, 1978.

[12] D. J. Cosgrove, and D. M. Durachko, "Automated pressure probe for measurement of water transport properties of higher plant cells." Review of Scientific Instrument. v.57. n.10. p.2614-2619, 1986.

[13] V. Bertucci Neto, Modelagem e automação em nova técnica de medida para relações de água e planta. (Modeling and automation in a new measurement technique for water and plant relationships.) Eng. PhD Thesis. Escola de Engenharia de São Carlos, Departamento de Engenharia Elétrica. 2005.

[14] P. Christofolleti "Material de aula (AgroAdvance)" (Classroom material (AgroAdvance)). 35pp, 2021.

[15] T. L. C. Andrade, Ação acaricida do hexythiazox, dicofol e óxido de fenbutatin, em três níveis de pH da calda, no controle do ácaro Brevipalpus phoenicis Geijskes, em condições de laboratório. (Acaricidal action of hexythiazox, dicofol and fenbutatin oxide, at three pH levels of the syrup, in the control of the mite Brevipalpus phoenicis Geijskes, under laboratory conditions.) Jaboticabal, 71 p. Dissertação (Mestrado em Agronomia, Área de Concentração em Entomologia Agrícola)

– Faculdade de Ciências Agrárias e Veterinárias, Universidade Estadual Paulista, 1997.

[16] D. M. Sanchotene et al, "Influência de sais e do pH da água na eficiência de imazethapyr + imazapic no controle de arroz-vermelho" ("Influence of salts and water pH on the efficiency of imazethapyr + imazapic in controlling red rice."), Planta Daninha, v.25, p.415-419, 2007.

[17] S. J. P. Carvalho et al, "Eficácia e pH de caldas de glifosato após a adição de fertilizantes nitrogenados e utilização de pulverizador pressurizado por CO_2 (Efficacy and pH of glyphosate mixtures after the addition of nitrogen fertilizers and the use of a sprayer pressurized by CO_2.)". Pesquisa Agropecuária Brasileira, 44, no.6: 569-575, 2009.

[18] U. R. Antuniassi, P. Miller, and M. Paice, Performance evaluation of injection metering systems, RevistaBrasileira de Engenharia Agrícola e Ambiental, Vol. 6, Issue 1, pp. 159-165, 2002.

[19] K. P. Gillis, D. K. Giles, D. C. Slaughter, and D. Downey, Injection mixing system for boomles, target-activated herbicide spraying, Transaction of the ASAE, Vol. 46, Issue 4, pp. 997-1008, 2003.

[20] Microchip Technology. http://www.microchip.com. accessed in 15/03/2023

A Model Based Intelligent Sensor to Control Sprinklers in Spray Actions

Deniver R. Schutz*,†, Elmer A. G. Peñaloza*,‡, Mercaldi Heitor V. *,§, Vilma A. Oliveira†, Paulo E. Cruvinel*

*Embrapa Instrumentation
Brazilian Agricultural Research Corporation, São Carlos, SP, Brazil
† Department of Electrical and Computer Engineering
University of São Paulo, São Carlos, SP, Brazil
‡ Department of Control and Automation Engineering
Engineering Center, Federal University of Pelotas, Pelotas, RS, Brazil
§ Department of Electrical Engineering
Federal University of São Carlos, São Carlos, SP, Brazil
Email: eagpenaloza@ufpel.edu.br, heitor@ufscar.br, deniver@usp.br, voliveira@usp.br, paulo.cruvinel@embrapa.br

Abstract—**Application of pesticides in crops is used to achieve food production. The use of technologies has become possible to decrease not only the biological risk but also the ecological and human ones that may occur during the application of pesticides. When using large sprayer machines, risks increase considerably due to the complexity of the trajectories required to cover the entire crop area. In this context, it is required a better analysis of the effects of different maneuvers on the quality and efficiency of the spray. This paper presents an intelligent control system based on models and smart sensors for automatic spray tip operation that enables error corrections as a function of the boom trajectory. As a new technology, such intelligent control and topology allow to increase quality and efficiency of the application of pesticides by agricultural sprayers.**

***Keywords*—*Intelligent sensor*; *electronic control*; *GPC*; *spray quality*.**

I. Introduction

In the last years, the concepts of precision agriculture and agriculture 4.0 has been the basis for novel methodologies for the application of technologies in most agricultural processes. Advanced automatic control units and the use of adequate instruments (sensors and actuators) increase production efficiency. In [1] an intelligent sensor is proposed to detect the concentration of agrochemicals at the exit of the spray nozzles for a sprayer with a direct agrochemical injection system. The intelligent sensor is mounted near the spray nozzles to measure the concentration response time, which uses a highly stable sinusoidal excitation signal. The results showed that the use of the intelligent sensor reduces the delay time errors produced by injecting agrochemicals near the output of the sprayer pump. With the assistance of the mounted sensor and an adequate control strategy, the appropriate concentration value for the application can be achieved.

Monitoring, failure detection, and automatic calibration of sensors and actuators have also been proposed. Systems with the ability to detect failures and make calibration settings are important, since working with agricultural machinery in the field is subject to great vibrations and critical climatic conditions. In this sense, the methodology presented in [2] supports the construction of a sensor virtual calibration module for agricultural sprayers. Such module for virtual calibration makes possible to validate the calibration of sensors operational conditions in real time of commercial sprayers, for instance, pressure, flow, temperature. Therefore, allowing to checkup if the sensor's operational procedures are or not correct.

On the other hand, advanced automatic control strategies allow to achieve a high degree of precision in the appropriate application of agrochemicals. In the work developed in [3] an intelligent fuzzy-Generalized Predictive Control (GPC) for Agricultural Sprayers is used. Thus, the authors use a predictive controller to advance control actions based on the delay dynamics of the hydraulic circuit of the agricultural sprayers. Among the results obtained in [3] it can be highlighted that the use of controllers based on predictive approaches increase the robustness in the presence of variations in the parameters of the sprayer.

This work proposes an intelligent automatic control strategy to improve production efficiency and quality. In this context, in Section II the key concepts of quality and efficiency of variable rate application are presented. Additionally, application examples are presented for each of these basic concepts. In the sequence, in Section III, the results and analysis about the use of new methodologies and technologies relevant in the area, are presented. Finally, in Section IV the conclusions of the work are reported.

II. Application of Advanced Model Control, Actuators and Sensors

In agricultural sprayers, there are two main concerns, the first is related to the quality of the application to maintain uniformity in the size of drops that are sprayed and the second is efficiency to eliminate errors related to volume and application rate.

A. *Quality of the Application*

There are climatic and geographical factors that can drastically affect the quality of an application. Factors such as wind speed, terrain slopes, and temperature differences can cause errors in the spectrum of drops in the powder applications. On the other hand, the operating conditions of agricultural machinery for each application affect quality. Factors such as the application speed V_p in $[km/h]$, pressure Δ_p in $[bar]$ and flow of the hydraulic circuit of the sprayer Q_p in $[\ell/min]$, the geometry of the spray nozzle and exit velocity in nozzle V_l in $[m/s]$ have direct effect on the spectrum of drops delivered.

The quality of the drops spectrum is measured from median diameters that define each of the characteristics of the spectrum (statistical moments of a probabilistic distribution). External factors such as climatic conditions and the topographic slop of the terrain impact the spectrum of drops [4] [5] [6]. Data obtained in laboratory allowed the development of models and definition of a quality description vector [7] [8]. Among the most used quality description are the Volumetric Mean Diameter (VMD), Sauter Mean Diameter (SMD), Relative Amplitude (RA) and diameter of droplets D_{01} and D_{09} that represents 10% and 90% of the total volume of liquid is in drops of smaller diameter, respectively. All these descriptors are organized in a quality vector where each one is characterized in $[\mu\text{m}]$ [8]. From advanced analytical models, valuable information on the effect of the operating conditions on the drops spectrum can be obtained. In this sense, in Figure 1 is observed the influence of the diameter of the output hole, for different orifice values d_0 of the full cone nozzles models CH0.5, CH1, CH3 and CH6, produced by MAGNOJET,® on the spray cone angles for pressure and flow established conditions [9] [10]. Thus, the strong effect on the spray cone angle can be observed from the variation of the hole diameter over a defined pressure.

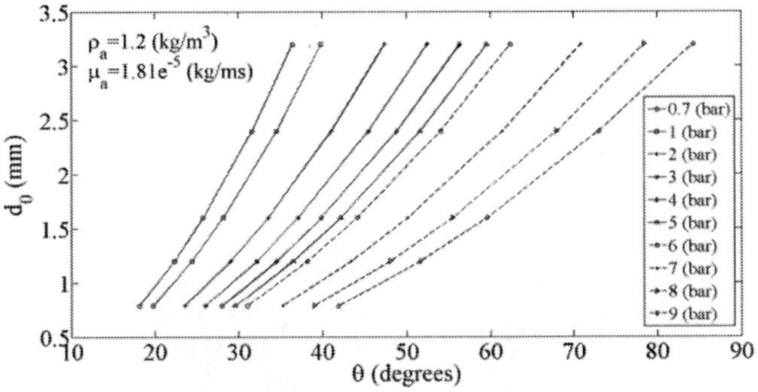

Figure 1. Relationship between the diameter of the nozzle orifice d_o and the cone angle θ for a full cone spray nozzle, simulated for different values of pressure Δ_p, for full cone nozzle.

Based on correlation analysis, each operation condition and quality parameters were compared as shown in Table I. It is observed that the pressure in the nozzle has a negative correlation with most of the proposed quality descriptors. Thus, the pressure is quite negatively correlated with the VMD (-0.61), with the $D_{0.1}$ (-0.54), SMD (-0.50), $D_{0.9}$ (-0.49) and Application Rate AR (-0.46). Besides, the pressure has a small correlation with the Covered Area CA (-0.26) and it is not correlated with the Relative Amplitude RA (-0.00). It is also important to highlight the strong negative correlation of the pressure with the other two operating conditions d_0 (-0.71) and V_p (-0.62) and this is a good indicator that the data obtained represent in a good way the hydraulic process for the production of droplets for full cone nozzles.

On the other hand, the velocity of application V_p has a high positive correlation with the VMD (0.80), the diameter $D_{0.9}$ (0.75), the application rate AR (0.71), Covered Area CA (0.66), the diameter $D_{0.1}$ (0.60) and SMD (0.53). Accordingly, just like the pressure of the nozzles, the speed of application has a fundamental effect on the quality descriptors. Therefore, the correlation analysis determines the relationship between the operating conditions and the statistical moments that determine the quality of the application. This analysis serves as a decision-making basis for intelligent control strategies, once it characterizes the positive or negative effect of the operating conditions on the quality vector.

B. Application Efficiency

The efficiency is determined by biological factors related to pests, harmful plants and the type of culture that attacks. Frequently the prescription of agrochemical type and concentration as well the nozzle type is carried out by a specialist, is given by the Application Rate (AR) in $[\ell/ha]$ [11]. Thus, efficiency is related to obtaining the appropriate AR value for each treatment. In this sense, external and internal factors can affect efficiency, leading to an AR error. As main internal factors that can lead to an erroneous AR are capacity of the sprayer to flow and pressure regulation and as a external factor, the curvilinear maneuvers that the agricultural machinery executes can lead to a relevant increase in AR errors. The study of the effect of curved maneuvers on agricultural production processes has been widely studied [12]. The kinematics on a curved path, Figure 2, show that are different speeds for each position of the nozzles on the sprayer boom, that is, velocity reduction for nozzles that are in the inner side of the curve (Left boom) .

Simulation environments, based on sprayer kinematic movement models, allow determinining the effect of curvilinear maneuvers present in real fields as well serving as a basis for decision-making in the agricultural spraying process. In Figure 3 the effect of curved trajectories on the pulverization error calculated from the Application Rate (AR) was observed. The results obtained through simulations showed the need for individual regulation of the flow in the spray nozzles, in order to compensate for the effects of the curvilinear path.

A feasible solution is the use of solenoid valves commanded by a voltage in the coil that mechanically opens and closes the valve. In Figure 4 a diagram inside a solenoid valve and a set of solenoid valves used for agricultural spray are shown. The internal operation of the solenoid valve (see Figure 4a) is as follows: in the closed step, the plunger (4) does not allow fluid to pass from the inlet (1) to the outlet (2) when solenoid coil (5) is energized by connectors and in the open step, the return spring (3) moves the plunger until the equilibrium position, allowing fluid to pass from the inlet to the outlet.

TABLE I
CORRELATION COEFFICIENTS BETWEEN THE QUALITY DESCRIPTORS AND OPERATING CONDITIONS OF THE AGRICULTURAL SPRAYING PROCESS.

Correlation analysis for quality descriptors and operating conditions ($n = 280$)										
	Δ_p	V_p	d_0	CA	AR	RA	VMD	$D_{0.1}$	$D_{0.9}$	SMD
Δ_p	1.00									
V_p	-0.62	1.00								
d_0	-0.71	0.99	1.00							
CA	-0.26	0.66	0.63	1.00						
AR	-0.46	0.71	0.72	0.89	1.00					
RA	-0.00	0.32	0.28	0.40	0.24	1.00				
VMD	-0.61	0.80	0.81	0.70	0.88	0.25	1.00			
$D_{0.1}$	-0.54	0.60	0.63	0.53	0.83	-0.05	0.84	1.00		
$D_{0.9}$	-0.49	0.75	0.75	0.62	0.77	0.45	0.84	0.70	1.00	
SMD	-0.50	0.53	0.55	0.48	0.64	-0.16	0.76	0.65	0.29	1.00

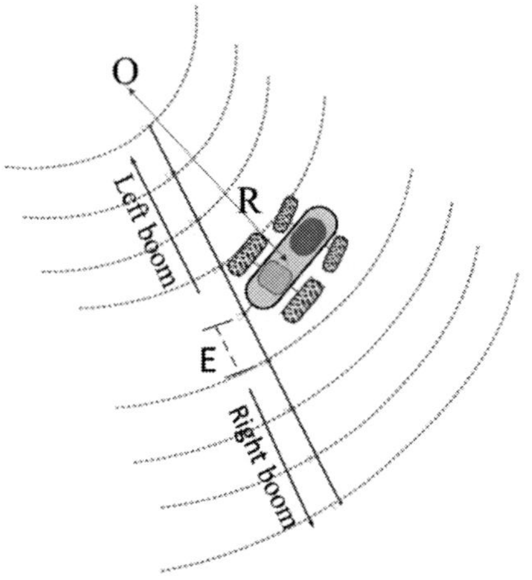

Figure 2. Curved path in which each nozzle has a relative speed which varies according to its position and the curve radius R in relation to the reference point O (figure extracted from [9])

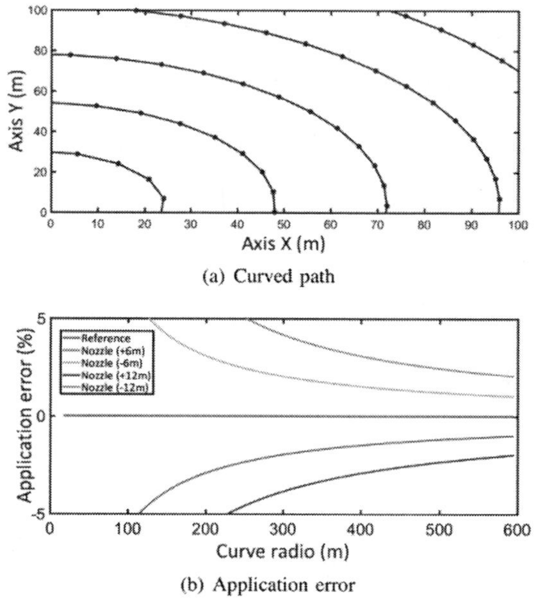

Figure 3. Kinematics simulation environment for the agricultural sprayer. (a) Path designed to evaluate the performance of the agricultural sprayer in curvilinear trajectories. (b) Application error in relation to the radius of the curvilinea trajectory.

For turbulent flow, the relationship between pressure and flow of the main components of the hydraulic circuit such as valves, pipes, spray nozzles and hoses is given by the relation $\Delta P = K_q Q_p^2$, where K_q is the fluidic resistance. This information is important, since changing the spray tips varies the hydraulic resistance of the system. Therefore, the change of spray nozzles can be used to control or regulate the pressure or flow of the system. The fluidic resistance ratio for three different types of standard flat fan nozzles, used for herbicides application,(models 11003, 11002, and 11015 of the brand Arag®) is shown in Table II [12]. It is important to note that the results shown in this section are carried out with different nozzle models in relation to those used in subsection II-A. Which does not invalidate the control topology purposed in this work, but requires additional experimentation to adjust the models and algorithms in order to achieve high levels of application quality and efficiency. To observe the effect that the switching (variation of fluidic resistance in Table II) of the tips in the pressure and flow, two lateral spray booms were equipped with 14 tips each, nozzle model 422WRC11002, and the set of solenoid valves with 4 tips (V1 to V4), nozzle model 422WRC11005, was mounted on the central spray boom.

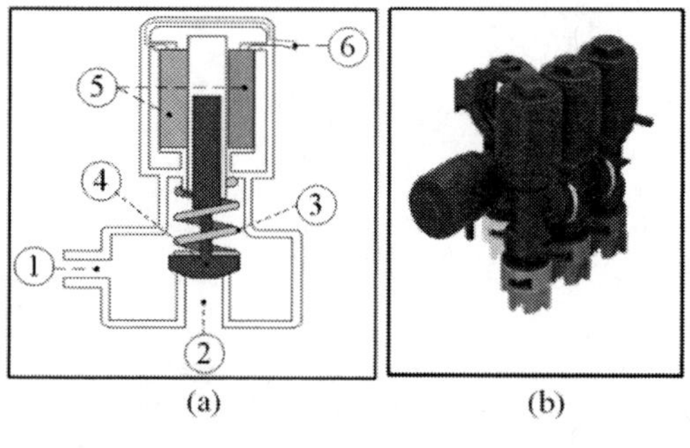

Figure 4. Individual control system for each spray nozzle. (a) Electromechanical system of the solenoid valve (b) Solenoid valves set (model QJS, Teejet®) and nozzles (model ASJ WRC, Arag®) (Figures adapted from [12])

From this information, intelligent nozzle selection strategies can be implemented for opening and closing solenoid valves

TABLE II
SET OF NOZZLES COMBINATIONS AND THE RESPECTIVE FLUIDIC RESISTANCES

	Nozzle model 422WRC			
	11003	11002	11015	
Q_{min}[l/min]	0.98	0.65	0.49	
Q_{max}[l/min]	1.39	0.92	0.69	
j	Active nozzles			$K_q(j)$
0	0	0	0	∞
1	0	0	1	836.6
2	0	1	0	473.0
3	0	1	1	154.1
4	1	0	0	207.6
5	1	0	1	92.5
6	1	1	0	75.1
7	1	1	1	44.5

in a set. Thus, consider the following test configuration: a sampling period of 50 ms, the solenoid valve is kept activated for 10 seconds and the data for two pressures, 100 and 200 kPa are colect. After the implementation of an intelligent algorithm, which properly choose the solenoid valves that must be activated, an appropriate nozzle switching sequence is obtained as shown in the Table III [12].

TABLE III
SEQUENCE OF TESTS USED FOR ACTIVATING THE SOLENOID VALVES DENOTED $V_k, k = 1,2,3,4$

State	Active valves	Time (s)
1	None	10
2	V_1	10
3	V_1 and V_2	10
4	V_1, V_2 and V_3	10
5	V_1, V_2, V_3 and V_4	10
6	V_2, V_3 and V_4	10
7	V_3 and V_4	10
8	V_4	10
9	None	10

The results of this smart switching strategy, based on independent actuators for each nozzle, can be observed in Figure 5. For each fixed pressure, it was possible to obtain four different values of flow rates, totalizing 8 possible states. In addition, it is observed that in the experiment performed when there is no switching of any spray nozzle (all closed), the hydraulic pressure of the system did not increased exponentially. This fact is because in the experiment, there are two other open spray booms that perform this hydraulic compensation. It is important to emphasize that when using actuators distributed to the sprayer bar, it allows to control the flow values (maintaining the desired AR) and additionally, it allows to regulate the pressure in adequate values (maintaining uniformity in the size of drops). Thus, it is observed that intelligent control strategies and high precision actuators, allow automatic control with great accuracy and therefore, increases the AR range without any human intervention.

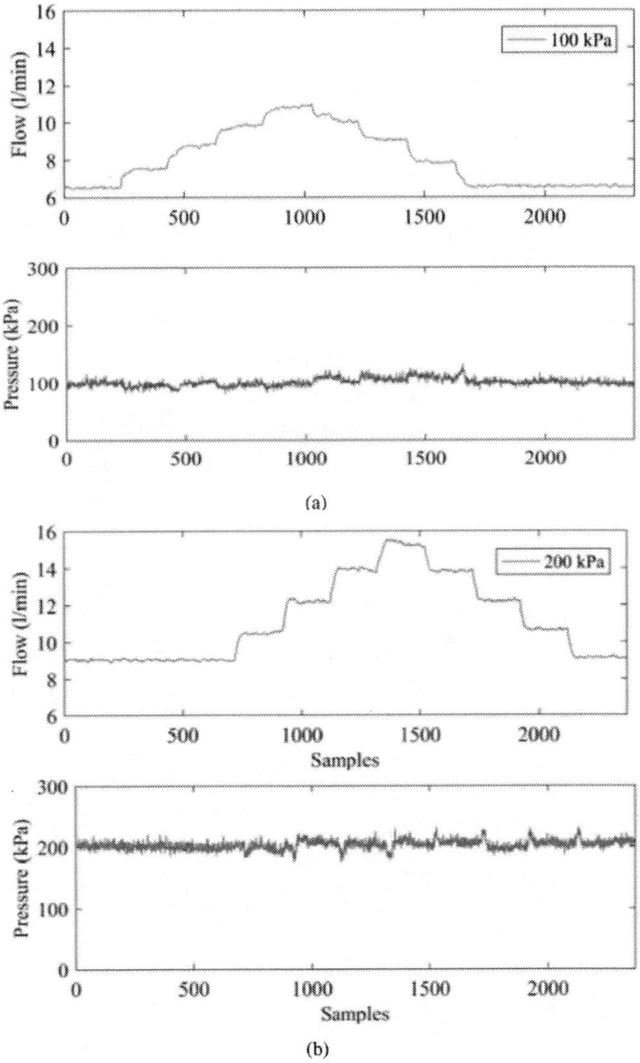

Figure 5. Pressure and flow rates obtained with the valve sequence according to Table III. (a) In the first test the pressure is maintained at 100 kPa. (b) In the second test the pressure is maintained at 200 kPa.

III. RESULTS AND DISCUSSIONS

Based on the new concepts, methods and technological devices, presented in this work, the need to create intelligent systems that can execute actions precise and efficiently in agricultural sprayers is observed. In this context, intelligent automatic control strategies must be implemented, which are based on the two approaches studied: the quality and efficiency of the application, in order to obtain a new hybrid implementation methodology.

The use of predictive control techniques (intelligent controller) together with information on application quality, obtained through an expert system, allows the design of new controllers topology for use in agricultural sprayers in the form presented in Figure6. This topology is divided into two main layers, one related to the intelligent controller and another related to a specialist system. The control layer is based on predictive control techniques (C) and the plant model (G) which must consider the delay time of the dynamics of the process. In this context, the use of a conductivity sensor allows to evaluate the delay time in direct agrochemical injection systems for various operating conditions of an agricultural sprayer. Information on the delay time is generally not used in real time control due to its intrinsic relationship with past events, but its modeling based on the variables measured in the sprayer allows its incorporation into an algorithm of anticipation of references increasing the accuracy of the application [13].

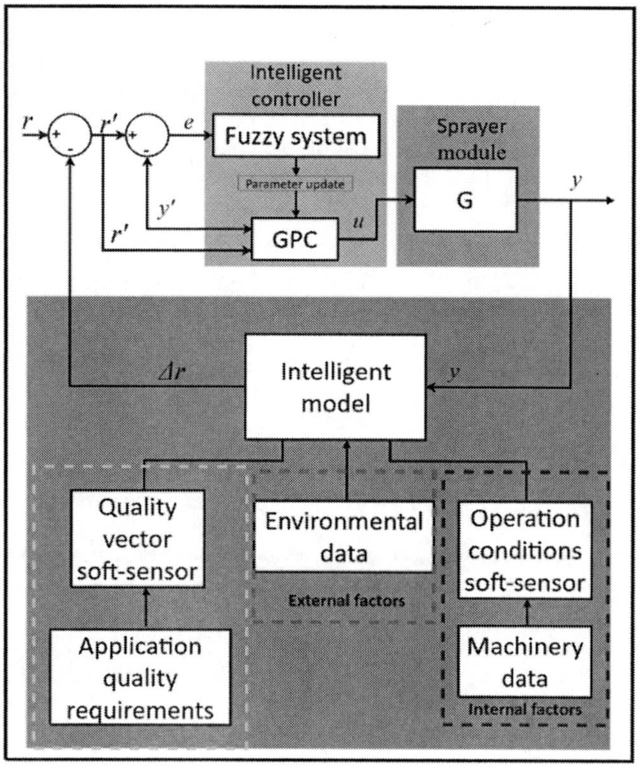

Figure 6. New intelligent control topology for increased quality and efficiency of variable rate application.

On the other hand, in the proposed topology, there is a layer based on a specialist system. At this stage of execution, intelligent models, based on the historical data, are developed to deliver additional information (Δr) to adjust the reference (r) for the control loop [8]. These reference values are delivered as output and are calculated from data from the machine (internal factors) and data from the environment where the application (external factors) is performed. In the topology, this data base is related to the requirements (quality vector values) of application quality. Thus, from this type of architectures, a balance between the efficiency and the quality of the variable rate application for agricultural sprayers is obtained.

IV. Conclusions

The use of new technologies based on advanced models, intelligent sensors and actuators, as well as adequate automatic control strategies, allow to achieve quality and efficiency in the application of agrochemicals. With the use of these technologies, a reduction in human and ecological risks related to this type of agribusiness processing can be achieved.

It is important to highlight that the integration of movement dynamics of agricultural machinery into intelligent control systems allows the evaluation of complex field situations and offers knowledge bases to execute actions to mitigate their effects.

The use of intelligent topologies for control allowed to perform efficient actions for pesticide variable rate application. Additionally, the intelligent system can offer adequate conceptual bases to perform decision-making processes to aggregate quality during spraying, which may bring improvements to pest control into a crop region.

References

[1] H. V. Mercaldi, C. H. Fujiwara, E. A. G. Penaloza, V. A. de Oliveira, and P. E. Cruvinel, "Smart and customized electrical conductivity sensor for measurements of the response time from sprayers based on direct injection," in *Sensors Transducers Journal*, ser. Sensor Device Technologies and Applications, vol. 193, no. 10. Barcelona, Spain: IFSA, 2015, pp. 1–10.

[2] P. B. Andrade, P. E. Cruvinel, and E. A. Peñaloza, "Module for virtual calibration of sensors of agricultural spraying systems (temperature, pressure and flow) using an arduino-based architecture and a controller area network bus (can)," in *2018 IEEE 12th International Conference on Semantic Computing (ICSC)*, 2018, pp. 352–357.

[3] D. R. Schutz, H. V. Mercaldi, E. A. G. Penaloza, V. A. Oliveira, and P. E. Cruvinel, "An intelligent fuzzy-gpc control for agricultural sprayers: Comparison between GPC and PID fuzzy controllers," in *CONTROLO 2022*, L. Brito Palma, R. Neves-Silva, and L. Gomes, Eds. Cham: Springer International Publishing, 2022, pp. 272–284.

[4] W. A. Sirignano, *Fluid Dynamics and Transport of Droplets and Sprays*. Cambridge: Cambridge University Press, 1999.

[5] A. Lefebvre, *Atomization and Sprays*, ser. Combustion, Hemisphere Publishing Corporation. Boca Raton, FL, USA: Taylor & Francis, 1988.

[6] H. M. Hanna and B. Steward, "Soil loading effects of planter depth-gauge wheels on early corn growth," *Applied Engineering in Agriculture*, vol. 26, no. 4, pp. 551–556, 2010.

[7] Y. Suzumura and P. E. Cruvinel, "Analysis of the quality of the efficiency of agricultural spraying with image processing and neural networks," *Sinergia*, vol. 6, no. 2, pp. 129–137, 2005.

[8] E. A. G. Peñaloza, V. A. Oliveira, and P. E. Cruvinel, "Using soft sensors as a basis of an innovative architecture for operation planning and quality evaluation in agricultural sprayers," *Sensors*, vol. 21, no. 4, 2021.

[9] E. A. G. Peñaloza, P. E. Cruvinel, V. A. Oliveira, and A. G. F. Costa, "A model approach to infer the quality in agricultural sprayers supported by knowledge bases and experimental measurements," *International Journal of Semantic Computing*, vol. 11, no. 03, pp. 279–292, 2017.

[10] R. F. Q. Magossi, E. A. G. Peñaloza, S. P. Battachharya, V. A. Oliveira, and P. E. Cruvinel, "Using the measurement-based approach to emulate the behavior of a sensor for internal hydraulic pressure drop measurements of sprayers in the agricultural industry," in *ALLSENSORS 2017: The Second International Conference on Advances in Sensors, Actuators, Metering and Sensing*. Nice, France: IARIA, Mar. 2017, pp. 10–15.

[11] J. Campos, M. Gallart, J. Llop, P. Ortega, R. Salcedo, and E. Gil, "On-farm evaluation of prescription map-based variable rate application of pesticides in vineyards," *Agronomy*, vol. 10, no. 1, 2020.

[12] H. V. Mercaldi, E. A. Peñaloza, R. A. Mariano, V. A. Oliveira, and P. E. Cruvinel, "Flow and pressure regulation for agricultural sprayers using solenoid valves," *IFAC-PapersOnLine*, vol. 50, no. 1, pp. 6607–6612, 2017, 20th IFAC World Congress.

[13] K. Romero Felizardo, H. Vinícius Mercaldi, P. Estevão Cruvinel, V. Alves Oliveira, and B. L Steward, "Modeling and model validation of a chemical injection sprayer system," *Applied Engineering in Agriculture*, vol. 32, no. 3, pp. 285–297, 2016.

New Design for a Thermo-formed Piezoelectret-based Accelerometer

Igor Nazareno Soares
Department of Electrical and Computer Engineering
Engineering School of São Carlos - University of São Paulo
São Carlos, Brazil
igor.soares@usp.br

Ruy Alberto Corrêa Altafim
Department of Electrical and Computer Engineering
Engineering School of São Carlos - University of São Paulo
São Carlos, Brazil
altafim@usp.br

Ruy Alberto Pisani Altafim
Department of Computer Systems and Informatics
Federal University of Paraíba
João Pessoa, Brazil
altafim@gmail.com

João Paulo Pereira do Carmo
Department of Electrical and Computer Engineering
Engineering School of São Carlos - University of São Paulo
São Carlos, Brazil
jcarmo@sc.usp.br

César Domingues
Department of Electrical and Computer Engineering
Engineering School of São Carlos - University of São Paulo
São Carlos, Brazil
cesard@sc.usp.br

Rogério Andrade Flauzino
Department of Electrical and Computer Engineering
Engineering School of São Carlos - University of São Paulo
São Carlos, Brazil
raflauzino@usp.br

***Abstract*—The article discusses the development and analysis of a new design for piezoelectric accelerometers that are used to measure acceleration in various applications. The new design uses piezoelectret materials, which offer advantages over traditional piezoelectric ones, including improved resistance to humidity, greater stability in extreme temperatures, and increased flexibility in meeting design requirements. The piezoelectret used in this study is a thermo-formed piezoelectret based on open-tubular channel structures. The paper explains the manufacturing process of the piezoelectret, which involves thermal lamination of two fluoroethylene propylene (FEP) foils and a polytetrafluoroethylene (PTFE) template, resulting in four open-tubular channels separated by a distance of 1.4 mm. The polymer structure is coated with aluminum through evaporation to create electrodes. The piezoelectret sample is then used to create a new design of accelerometers with a single detection axis, consisting of a cylindrical lead seismic mass enclosed in a PTFE sheath placed over the piezoelectret. An elastic component made of polyurethane foam provides mechanical support and restitution. The authors conclude that this new design of piezoelectric accelerometers using piezoelectret materials has the potential to offer superior performance in various applications.**

Keywords—accelerometer, piezoelectret

I. Introduction

Accelerometers are widely used for measuring acceleration in various industrial, medical, and scientific applications. These accelerometers convert acceleration into an electrical signal, enabling the analysis and interpretation of the dynamic characteristics of a moving system. Since their invention in the 1950s, piezoelectric accelerometers have been fundamental tools for engineers and researchers in fields such as vibration analysis, process control, health monitoring, and structural testing [1].

In recent years, a new technology has emerged in the development of accelerometers: piezoelectret materials. These polymeric materials offer several advantages over traditional piezoelectric materials, including greater stability in extreme temperatures, improved resistance to humidity, and increased flexibility to meet different design requirements. Since 2004, Sessler and collaborators have provided an overview of this emerging technology, including the manufacture of piezoelectret accelerometers and methods for producing sensors with superior performance [2] [3]. In 2009, Altafim Pisani and collaborators [4] [5] developed a new piezoelectret material, named thermo-formed piezoelectrets, which presents a high piezoelectric coefficient with the same advantages of piezoelectrets. They also demonstrated that this material has a linear behavior with frequency until the frequency of 30 kHz, where a resonance peak occurs, which can be modified by the geometry of the channels [6]. In the following sections, we present and analyze a novel design of accelerometers utilizing this material. For instance, Section 2 describes the production of the piezoelectret and the accelerometer, including details on fabrication. In Section 3, significant results are presented and thoroughly discussed. Finally, in Section 4, we present our main conclusions.

II. Accelerometer design

A piezoelectret sample, as depicted in Figure 1, was fabricated using the thermal lamination technique described in [5]. In this process, two 50 μm-thick fluoroethylene propylene (FEP) foils were laminated at 300 °C with a 100 μm-thick polytetrafluoroethylene (PTFE) film placed between them. The PTFE was previously laser-cut with four rectangular openings through which the FEP films were bonded during lamination. After this process, the PTFE was removed, leaving an FEP structure with four open channels. The PTFE was designed to produce four channels that were 1.4 mm wide and 30 mm long, regularly spaced at intervals of 1.4 mm. The polymer film-like structure was later coated with aluminum through evaporation, creating electrodes with a final active area of 168 mm^2.

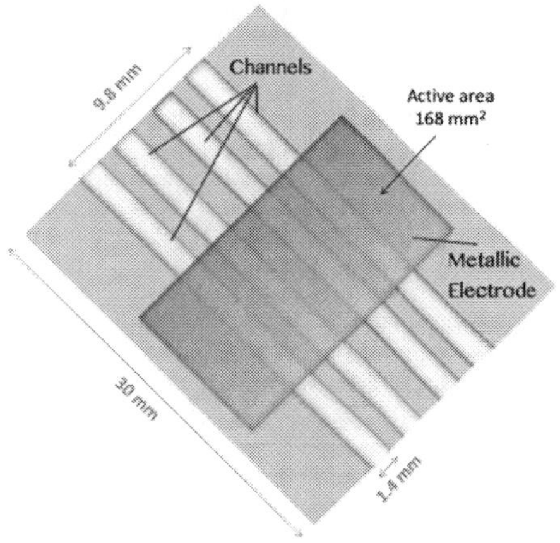

Fig. 1. Sample of Thermo-formed Piezoelectret with channels.

A. Description

Figure 2 depicts the schematic of the thermo-formed piezoelectret accelerometer (TFPA) with a single detection axis. The accelerometer is composed of a 30 g cylindrical lead seismic mass, with dimensions of 10 mm in height and 18 mm in diameter, enclosed within a PTFE sheath placed over a thermo-formed piezoelectret. An elastic component made of polyurethane foam with a density of 12 kg/m³ is placed on top of the mass to provide mechanical support and restitution, while an aluminum guide vertically guides the mass. To ensure mechanical resistance and electrical shielding, the transducer is connected to a BNC connector and is enclosed in an aluminum cylindrical case measuring 74 mm in height and 51 mm in diameter. This dimension is far larger than the standard accelerometer; however, it is expected that this design will be reduced by 10 times in the laboratory facilities.

For the tests conducted with the TFPA, a custom-made shaker was constructed using a 15.24 cm (6 inch) diameter mid-bass speaker from *Foxer Alto-falantes®*, equipped with a ferrite magnet and an aluminum single coil, with 4 Ω impedance, 80 W power, frequency response ranging from 30 Hz to 30 kHz, and sensitivity of 90 dB/W. An acrylic

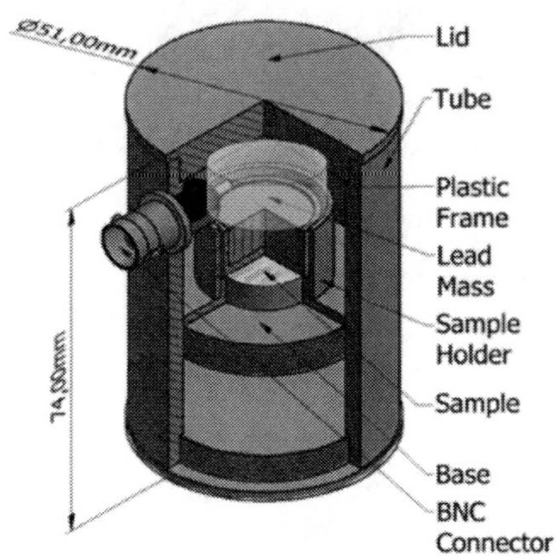

Fig. 2. New design of thermo-formed piezoelectret (TFPA) accelerometer, with polyurethane foam.

holder with a PTFE guide was fabricated to support the TFPA, as shown in Figure 3.

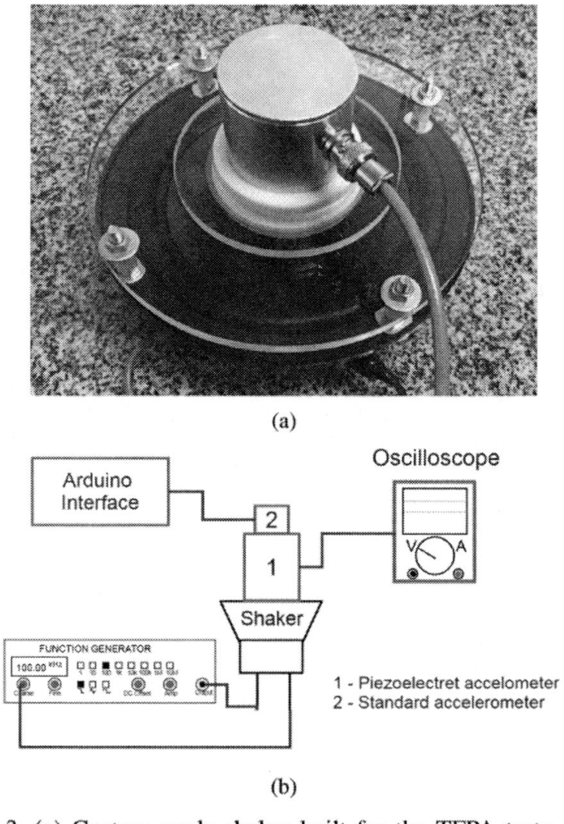

Fig. 3. (a) Custom-made shaker built for the TFPA tests. (b) Block diagram of the experimental setup.

An ADXL327 accelerometer from Analog Devices connected to an *Arduino UNO®* microcontroller board was used as reference measure. It has an acceleration input range of $\pm 2g$, sensitivity of 420 mV/g and frequency response from

0.5 Hz to 1600 Hz.

The input signals for the shaker were generated using the Tektronix function generator model AFG3022CA. A Taramps TL-500 Class D Amplifier was used for signal amplification.

III. Theoretical considerations

A simplified depiction of the thermo-formed piezoelectret accelerometer is presented in Figure 4 (a). As shown, the piezoelectret is placed under an enclosure seismic mass that compresses the piezoelectret channels when subjected to vibration.

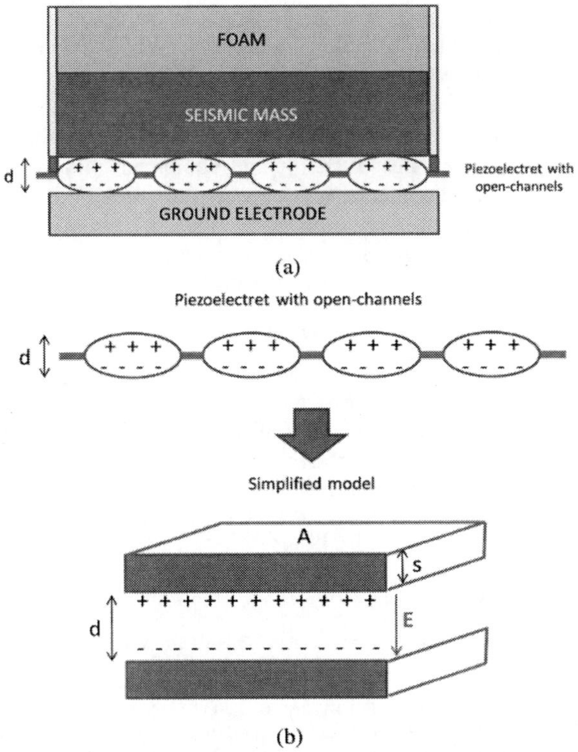

Fig. 4. (a) Cross-sectional view representation of the thermo-formed piezoelectret accelerometer. (b) Representation of the simplified model for a piezoelectret.

The piezoelectret compression results in a change in thickness (Δd) and subsequently leads to a voltage variation (ΔV) at the sample electrodes [8]. According to Sessler et al. [7], if the piezoelectret cavities is modeled as rectangular cavities, as shown in Figure 4 (b), then the voltage variation ΔV due to a variation Δd can be mathematically determined by Equation 1:

$$\Delta V = E.\Delta d \tag{1}$$

where E is the electric field inside an air cavity (here represented by the open channels), and given by Equation 2:

$$E = \frac{\sigma s}{\epsilon_0(\epsilon d + s)} \tag{2}$$

where σ is the superficial electric charge density of the cavity walls, s is the thickness of the polymeric film, ϵ_0 is the vacuum permittivity, and ϵ is the relative permittivity of the polymeric layer.

The term Δd from Equation 1 can be determined from Young's modulus of the cavity plus foam (Y) when a force F is applied to it, as shown below in Equation 3:

$$Y = \frac{F/A}{\Delta d/d} \implies \Delta d = \frac{Fd}{Y.A} \tag{3}$$

As F can also be expressed as $m_s\Delta a$, where m_s is the seismic mass and Δa is the acceleration, ΔV can be determined by Equation 4:

$$\Delta V = \frac{\sigma s}{\varepsilon_0(\varepsilon.d + s)} \cdot \frac{d}{Y.A} \cdot m_s\Delta a \tag{4}$$

Thus, in the piezoelectret accelerometer, any variation in acceleration (Δa) generates a voltage variation (ΔV).

IV. Results and Discussions

As previously described, the proposed accelerometer (TFPA) was tested over a shaker platform, which vibrated over frequencies ranging between 100 Hz to 1000 Hz. It´s output, recorded as peak-to-peak millivolts (mV) signals, provided the frequency response plot in Figure 5. The graph reveals a clear resonance peak at 200 Hz and a relatively linear response for frequencies above 400 Hz.

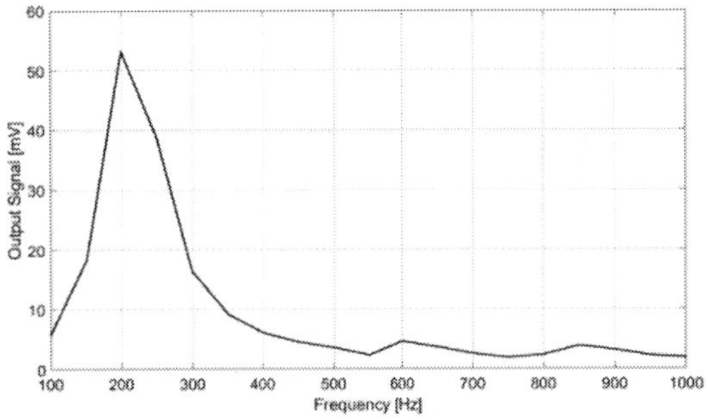

Fig. 5. Frequency response of TFPA output signal peak-to-peak voltage.

This result is analogous to the response obtained from a commercial accelerometer ADXL327 (depicted in Figure 6) under identical vibrating conditions. The comparison can be further elucidated by normalizing the values using their respective maximum peak-to-peak output voltage within the frequency range of the experiment, as shown in Figure 8, which have a correlation factor of 0,985.

Both the ADXL327 accelerometer and the TFPA exhibit a linear response within the same frequency range, suggesting that the 200Hz resonance may not be an inherent characteristic of the accelerometer but rather a consequence of the test system assembly used in the calibration procedure. Nevertheless, this system can still be utilized to determine the TFPA's

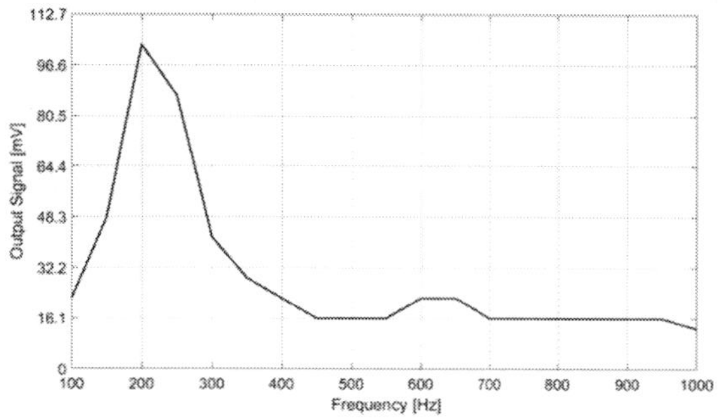

Fig. 6. Frequency response of ADXL327 reference accelerometer output signal peak-to-peak voltage.

sensitivity in mV/g, considering that the ADXL327 has a linear sensitivity of 420mV/g [9]. In such a case, dividing the data on the y-axis of Figure 6 by 420mV/g generates a graph of acceleration in m/s², shown in Figure 7. Furthermore, dividing the y-axis data of the graph in Figure 5 by the corresponding acceleration in m/s² for each frequency, Figure 7 allows us to determine an average sensitivity of 78mV/g for frequencies above 400Hz.

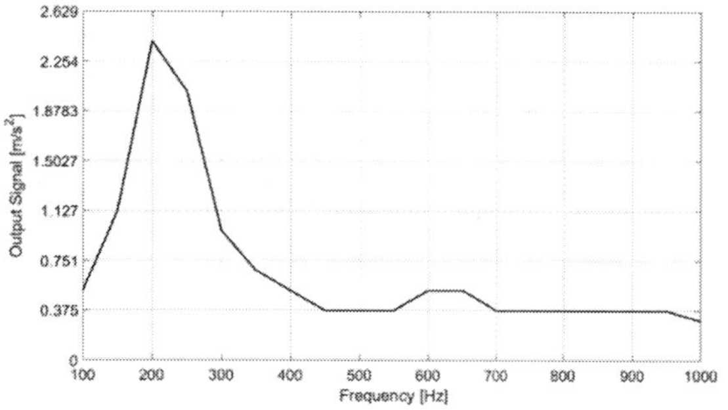

Fig. 7. Acceleration response of the system in $[m/s^2]$.

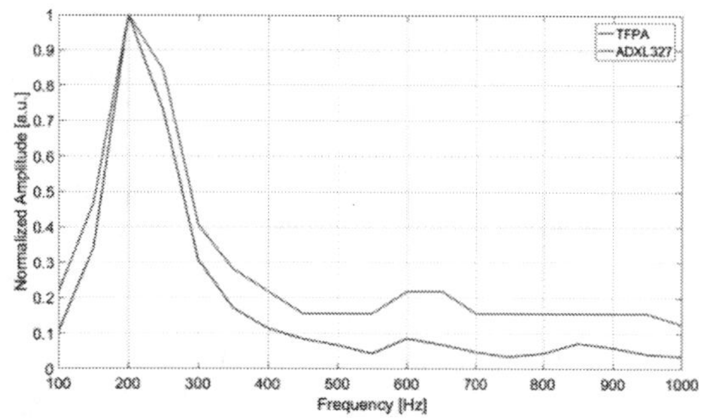

Fig. 8. Normalized frequency response of TFPA and ADXL327 reference accelerometer.

V. Conclusion

This article presents a novel approach for producing accelerometers using thermo-formed piezoelectrets. A brief description of the process for fabricating piezoelectrets with open channels is provided, followed by the construction of the accelerometer with a single detection axis. Some advantages of using FEP thermo-formed piezoelectrets over more traditional ones are emphasized, such as improved moisture resistance and thermal stability. Measurements in the frequency domain (up to 1 kHz) were performed and reported, allowing a comparison between the proposed accelerometer and a standard model (ADXL327). It was observed that both accelerometers presented a very similar response with a clear resonance peak at 200 Hz, which was attributed to the measuring setup. From this result, it was calculated that the TFPA presents a sensitivity of 78 mV/g while the commercial ADXL327 provides 420 mV/g. This discrepancy in sensitivity is related to the higher amplification gain and was not understood as a deficiency of the TFPA accelerometer. It was concluded that accelerometers with the proposed design, i.e., using piezoelectrets, can be explored in a variety of applications, especially in studies of motor and equipment vibrations. As for future developments, it is expected to reduce the physical dimensions of the accelerometer, extend the frequency range analysis to higher frequencies, and employ them in studies regarding motor mechanical vibrations.

Acknowledgement

The Brazilian funding agencies CAPES (Coordenação de Aperfeiçoamento de Pessoal de Nível Superior) and CNPq (Conselho Nacional de Pesquisa), Federal University of Paraíba, and University of São Paulo (Electrical and Computer Department at Engineering School of São Carlos).

References

[1] J. H. Simmons and R. F. Rangaswamy, "Piezoelectric accelerometer", Review of Scientific Instruments, vol. 31, no. 4, pp. 421-425, 1960, doi: 10.1063/1.1716642.

[2] J. Hillenbrand and G. M. Sessler, "Quasistatic and dynamic piezoelectric coefficients of polymer foams and polymer film systems", IEEE Transactions on Dielectrics and Electrical Insulation, vol. 11, no. 1, pp. 72-79, Feb. 2004, doi: 10.1109/TDEI.2004.1266319.

[3] J. Hillenbrand, M. Kodejska, Y. Garcin, H. V. Seggern and G. M. Sessler, "High-sensitivity piezoelectret-film accelerometers", IEEE Transactions on Dielectrics and Electrical Insulation, vol. 17, no. 4, pp. 1021-1027, August 2010, doi: 10.1109/TDEI.2010.5539670.

[4] R. A. C. Altafim et al., "Piezoelectrets from thermo-formed bubble structures of fluoropolymer-electret films", IEEE Transactions on Dielectrics and Electrical Insulation, vol. 13, no. 5, pp. 979-985, Oct. 2006, doi: 10.1109/TDEI.2006.247822.

[5] R. A. P. Altafim et al., "Template-based fluoroethylenepropylene piezoelectrets with tubular channels for transducer applications", Journal of Applied Physics, vol. 106, p. 014106, 2009, doi: 10.1063/1.3159039.

[6] R. A. P. Altafim et al., "Fluoropolymer piezoelectrets with tubular channels: resonance behavior controlled by channel geometry", Apply. Physics A, vol. 107, pp. 965–970, 2012, doi:10.1007/s00339-012-6848-z

[7] J. Hillenbrand, S. Haberzettl, T. Motz , and G. M. Sessler. "Electret Accelerometers: Physics and Dynamic Characterization." The Journal of the Acoustical Society of America 129.6 (2011): 3682-689. Web.

[8] G. M. Sessler, J. Hillenbrand, "Electromechanical response of cellular electret films", Applied Physics Letters, vol. 75 pp. 3405–3407, 1999.

[9] J. Tsai, K. Chen, S. Chen, Y. Liu and D. Lee, "Design of a Novel Sensing Module for Machine Tool Vibration Monitoring by Integrating Multiple MEMS Accelerometers", in: International Conference on Industrial Application Engineering 2018, pp. 250-256, 2018, doi: 10.12792/iciae2018.049.

An Interoperable Framework for Network-Enabled Cross-Border Multi-Agency First-Aid Vehicles in Multiple Casualty Incidents

Marco Manso
PARTICLE Summary
Lisbon, Portugal
e-mail: marco@particle-summary.pt

Alberto Montarelo
TASSICA
Madrid, Spain
e-mail: alberto.montarelo@tassica.com

Jorge Maestre Vidal
INDRA
Madrid, Spain
e-mail: jmaestre@indra.es

Pedro Petiz
PARTICLE Summary
Lisbon, Portugal
e-mail: pedro@particle-summary.pt

Navid Behzadi Koochani
Servicio de Urgencias Medicas de Madrid, Madrid, Spain
e-mail: navid.behzadi@salud.madrid.org

Meritxell Bassols Tayeda
INDRA
Madrid, Spain
e-mail: mbassols@indra.es

Bárbara Guerra
PARTICLE Summary
Lisbon, Portugal
e-mail: barbara@particle-summary.pt

Ioannis Chatzichristos
ARATOS
Athens, Greece
e-mail: ichatzichristos@aratos.gr

Sergio López Bernal
Universidad de Murcia
Murcia, Spain
e-mail: slopez@um.es

***Abstract*- A cross-border Multiple Casualty Incident (MCI) affects a large number of persons requiring urgent medical assistance by authorities and warrants significant international coordination. This work addresses the technical challenge of building a cross-border multi-agency coalition as a federated system supporting international coordination, while delivering the required assistance to the victims. Using as basis a reference MCI cross-border scenario, an overarching architecture is defined, the VALKYRIES architecture, including the rules, protocols and data models that enable integration of heterogeneous entities, being those services, applications or sensors. By implementing the VALKYRIES architecture, organisations become ready to participate in a federated collaborative environment, exchange MCI-related information and achieve high-levels of shared situational awareness, thus contributing towards a better employment of resources and improving the mission's effectiveness and efficiency.**

Keywords*- *Multiple casualty incident; Emergency Services; Interoperability; Federated System; Technical Architecture.

I. INTRODUCTION

A MCI affects a large number of persons requiring urgent medical assistance by authorities. It may demand more resources and capabilities than those available in a single organisation, thus collaborating with other agencies is fundamental to deliver an efficient response. This is even more so for incidents crossing borders, where international coordination is mandatory. Implementing a cross-border multi-agency coalition offers significant technology-related challenges, since different technological solutions, applications, communication networks, data models, and protocols – including legacy solutions – are used by the different involved partners, resulting in a heterogeneous landscape of artifacts and tools. Standards for interoperability, contributing towards the harmonisation between heterogeneous organisations, have to be defined, implemented and adopted.

This paper presents the work performed in the VALKYRIES Action towards defining rules and protocols enabling the integration of the different capabilities, technologies, data gathering sensors and artifacts at play in a cross-border MCI, in a coordinated and in-field deployable way. The paper is structured as follows: Section II describes an operating cross-border MCI scenario, including involved actors, artifacts and information flows; Section III presents the technical architecture defined for VALKYRIES, including relevant standards and defined services; Section IV introduces the data models used in VALKYRIES; and Section V concludes this paper.

II. OPERATING IN A MULTIPLE CASUALTY INCIDENT SCENARIO

The VALKYRIES Innovation Action analyses and defines harmonised mechanisms for the effective management and deployment of resources during the run-up to a major crisis related to any kind of cross-border disaster (natural or intentional) that demands the fast actuation and coordination of first-aid emergency services and associated response teams, with Civil-Military Cooperation (CIMIC) and volunteering. Its primary objective is to develop, implement, validate, and apply innovative theoretical foundations, methods, prototypes, and their demonstration on a reference integration framework to support the ongoing/planned European actions for pre-standardisation

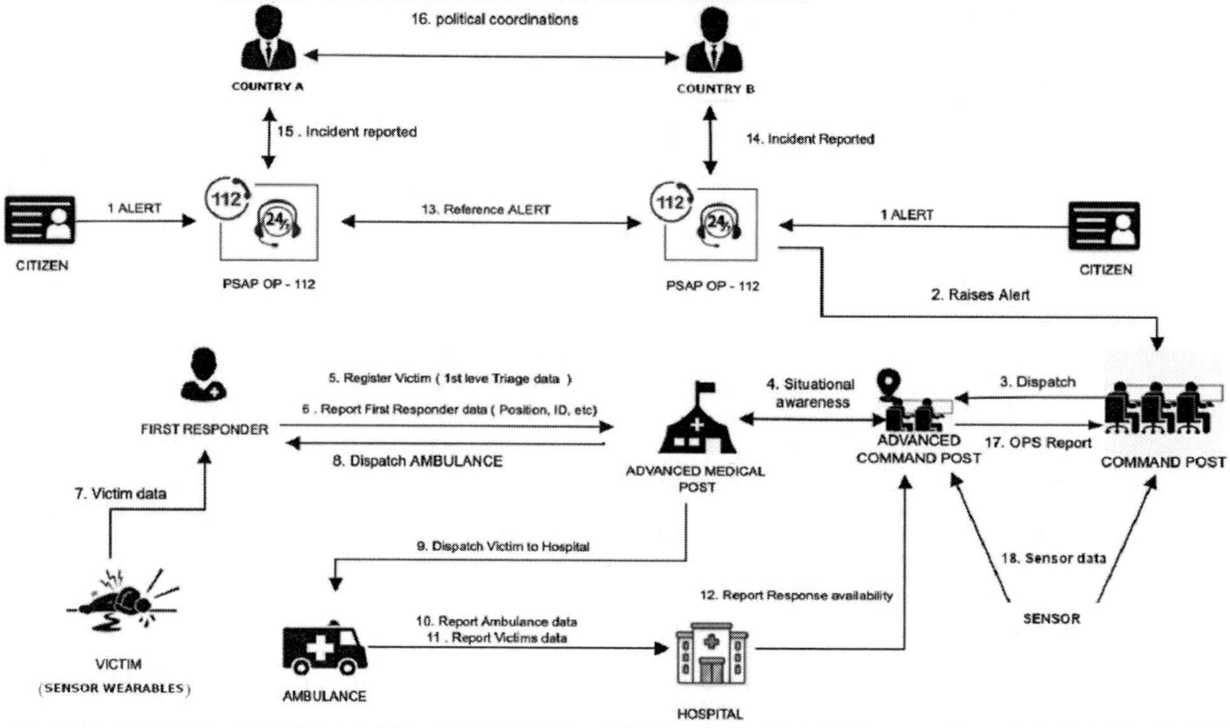

Figure 1. General Operating Scenario: Interaction Diagram

and harmonisation technologies, procedures, preparedness, and cross-border/sector cooperation for first aid response at disaster management by first aid emergency services, with the focus on health services and vehicular deployments.
VALKYRIES also aims to generate synergies between different parties, regardless of their language and action protocols, to optimize the management of the incident without trying to modify its structure and normal operation. By improving interoperability in cross-border and cross-sector emergency situations, particularly when involving a MCI, the reference integration framework will empower improved coordination and employment of resources and increased mission efficiency and effectiveness.

The project implements an Observe-Orient-Decide-Act (OODA) approach for solving the identified harmonisation challenges [1], where:

- Observe: Resembles the acquisition of preliminarily factual knowledge.
- Orient: Reasons on the best hypothetical approach for addressing identified gaps and materialise opportunities.
- Decide: Selects the most suitable harmonisation options and applies them on a reference integration framework.
- Act: Coincides with deploying, evaluating and contrasting the assumed hypothesis based on the achieved analytical and empirical results.

Next, a reference scenario is presented that will guide the definition of the VALKYRIES architecture.

A. *Reference Operating Scenario*

A MCI scenario involves multiple actors operating at different levels that need to interact with each other to develop shared situational awareness and ensure adequate coordination of resources.

A general overview of an operating scenario, showing the main involved actors and their interrelations, is depicted in Figure 1. The fictional scenario involves a large forest fire starting in the region of Badajoz, close to the border between Spain and Portugal. The fire rapidly spreads to the Natural Park of *Serra de S. Mamede* in Portugal, evolving into a cross-border incident. The intensity of the fire, together with the large extension of burned ground and weather conditions, cause the authorities to activate the regional emergency plan at both sides of the border. Authorities understand that, to minimise human and material damage, an effective collaboration is crucial. Cooperation is established at different levels, including political (e.g., ministries collaboration and protocols), tactical (civil protection authorities and command posts) and operational (e.g., firefighters, medical teams and their vehicles).

This fictional incident involves the deployment of several technological artifacts (presented in Table I) and information flows (presented in Table II).

TABLE I. ACTORS AND TECHNOLOGICAL ARTIFACTS

Actors	Technological Artifact
Citizens	User Terminal (e.g., Mobile phone and App), Web-client
Firefighters FR (*) Advanced Medical Post	Wearables (e.g., activity tracker with satellite positioning) User Terminal (e.g., Professional Mobile Phone with App) TETRA Terminal
PSAP (*) Operator 112 Coordination Centre	112 Terminal Emergency Management System
Coordination Centre Command Post	Emergency Management System Command and Control System
Political Liaison	User Terminal (e.g., Phone / E-mail)
First Aid Vehicles & Ambulances	Vehicle Terminal (with network connection and satellite positioning) Medical devices and wearables
Hospital	Hospital Information System
Victims	Medical devices and wearables

(*) PSAP: Public Safety Answering Point. FR: First Responder

III. VALKYRIES ARCHITECTURE AND APPROACH

Considering the large variety of involved actors and sovereignty over their own systems, VALKYRIES adopts a federated approach to connect the different systems together, a system of systems approach aiming to provide distributed operational response, coordination capability and supporting services. VALKYRIES overarching architecture is presented next.

A. *VALKYRIES Overarching Architecture*

The VALKYRIES overarching architecture follows a federated approach capable of interconnecting heterogeneous applications, data sources and systems. It establishes a common integrated framework (e.g., principles, business processes, core functions, data models, protocols, communications and security requirements), herein named as VALKYRIES Interoperability Framework (VIF). VIF encompasses: **federation-level data services** enabling data sharing among the different applications; **communications services** that establish the connectivity among the different users; and the **core services** that establishes common functions required for the orchestration and deployment of resources. Applications and services provided by each agency interoperate with each other via SIGRUN, a conceptual connector complying with VIF. A high-level diagram illustrating the VIF integration concept is presented in Figure 2.

TABLE II. INFORMATION FLOW

1. Alert	Communication of a medical emergency by a citizen via an emergency call
2. Raises Alert	Report of the emergency case to the Command Centre
3. Dispatch	Forward the emergency case to the Advanced Command Post in response to a confirmed incident
4. Situational Awareness	Report incident victims and medical status and data received, including victims, FR and assets' location status and priority
5. Register victim	Victim information including triage data
6. Report first response data	First responder information, including location and status
7. Victim data	Victim data update: symptoms, pathology, medical information; status (triage). Emergency case file updated
8. Dispatch Ambulance	Dispatch information: assign victim to an ambulance, victim information
9. Dispatch Victim to Hospital	Ambulance task, Destination hospital, victim information, Emergency case file updated; victim pathology
10. Report ambulance data	Ambulance position and time-of-arrival, victim information (on-transport)
11. Report victim data	Victim information; victim vitals data (ambulance or wearable devices); Victim triage update
12. Report response availability	Hospital medical emergency's availability
13. Reference Alert	Cross-border incident data alert
14. Incident Report (Spain)	Data on cross-border confirmed incidents generated from Spanish authorities
15. Incident Report (Portugal)	Data on cross-border confirmed incidents generated from Portuguese authorities
16. Political Coordination	National authorisations and political agreements
17. Operations Report	Operations' progress and status: incident updates; assets' updates; victims' updates; situational awareness of high risks elements
18. Sensor data	Deployed sensor data: weather, fire detection, air quality indicator, video, chemical/biological agents detection, beacon (location)

Within the VIF concept, applications and services are able to either natively implement VIF or, in case of legacy systems, a specifically connector may be applied. This ensures that the VALKYRIES concept can be universally applied to any application, data source and component, as illustrated in Figure 3.

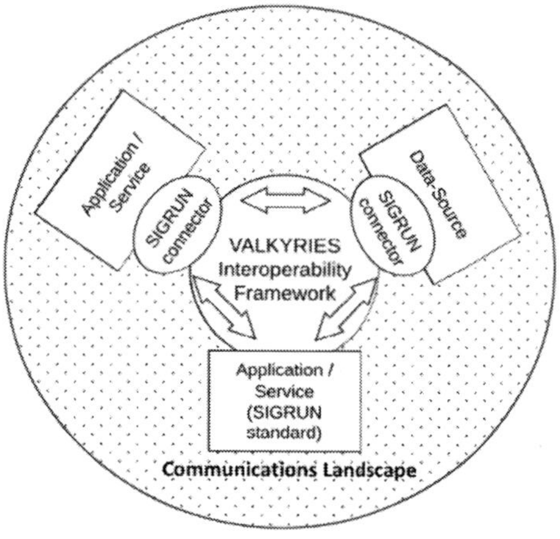

Figure 2. VIF Integration Concept Overview

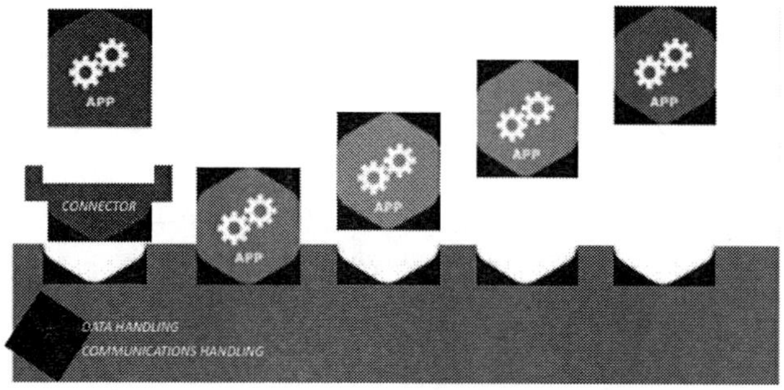

Figure 3. SIGRUN Integrations: native and connector-based

B. *Standards and Technologies for Interoperability*

VIF rules and principles were defined considering and benefiting from existing widely-used standards and technologies, presented next.

- **All-over-IP**: the Internet Protocol (IP) (RFC6864), is the current dominant network protocol, connecting billions of systems on the Internet. VIF uses IP to interconnect applications and services.
- **Emergency Data Exchange Language** (EDXL): the Organisation for the Advancement of Structured Information Standards (OASIS) sets the main goal of the EDXL as an enabler to facilitate emergency information sharing and data exchange among key stakeholders namely local, state actors, national agencies or non-governmental organisations supporting emergency response and management services [2].
- **EDXL Hospital Availability Exchange** (EDXL-HAVE) specifies an Extensible Markup Language (XML) document format that allows the communication of the status of a hospital, its services and resources, including bed capacity and availability, emergency department status, available service coverage, and the status of the hospital's facilities and operations [2].
- **NENA Emergency Incident Data Object** (EIDO): the United States' National Emergency Number Association (NENA) created EIDO, a standardised, industry-neutral format for exchanging emergency incident information between disparate manufacturer systems located within one or more public safety agencies, and with other incident stakeholders [3]. Recognising the existence of many functional elements involved in emergency management and response, which in turn involve multi-agencies and actors, EIDO provides a common representation of emergency incidents across the lifecycle of an emergency.
- **FHIR for medical data**: Fast Healthcare Interoperability Resources (FHIR) is a standard for healthcare data exchange, published by Health Level 7 (HL7) [4]. FHIR was created to cope with the fast digitisation of health records, aiming to provide a harmonised way to ensure that electronic health records and medical data are available, discoverable, and understandable across different medical agencies and healthcare systems.
- **Smart Applications REFerence ontology** (SAREF): under the aegis of the European Telecommunications Standards Institute (ETSI), SAFER is intended to enable interoperability between solutions from different providers and among various activity sectors in the Internet of Things (IoT) [5]. SAREF identified about 50 different semantic assets later translated into Web Ontology Language (OWL). SAREF is being extended to address specific sectors like agriculture, automotive, energy and environment.
- **VALKYRIES web-based requests**: components in VALKYRIES may need to issue requests to other federated components, such as retrieving a list of emergency incidents, retrieving information about the health status of a specific victim or even request the assignment of an ambulance to a victim. Federated components can issue web-based requests to other components using the widely adopted Representational State Transfer (REST) architectural style. REST emphasises scalability of component interactions, generality of interfaces, independent deployment of components, and intermediary components to reduce interaction latency, enforce security, and encapsulate legacy systems [6]. The application of REST principles with the Hypertext Transfer Protocol (Secure) (HTTP(S)) protocol (Request for Comments or RFC 7231) and JavaScript Object Notation (JSON)-formatted payload in web-based server-client architectures is widely used over the Internet. Servers expose their interfaces by what is called as "RESTful Application Programming Interfaces (APIs)".
- **Data exchange and communication protocols:** complementing transactional requests (i.e., RESTful API), VALKYRIES supports a message broker service following the publish-subscribe paradigm via the open standard Message Queuing Telemetry Transport (MQTT) version 5.0 [7]; data streaming via *Websockets* (Internet Engineering Task Force or IETF RFC 6455); video streaming via the Web Real-Time Communication (WebRTC*)* protocol suite [8]; and

multimedia communication via the Extensible Messaging and Presence Protocol (XMPP) standard (RFC 6120).

- **Security**: access to VALKYRIES is restricted to authorised users with valid credentials. Exchanged information is end-to-end encrypted, using Transport Layer Security (TLS). TLS is designed to prevent eavesdropping, tampering, and message forgery (RFC 8446).

C. *VIF Services*

VIF Services provide underlying functions that support the integration in the SIGRUN connector, enabling applications and services to become a part of the VALKYRIES federation. VIF Services are presented in Figure 4 and described next.

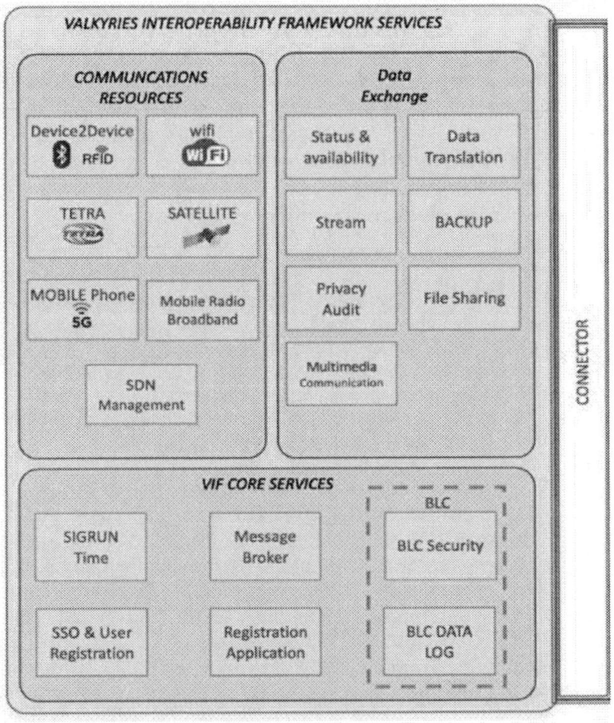

Figure 4. VIF Services.

VIF Services are organised in three categories:

Communication Resources: These services are responsible for delivering communication capabilities to federated entities, enabling them to access and interact with VALKYRIES resources. It also deals with management and coordination of different networks and technologies to deliver robust and resilient communications. It uses a Software Defined Network (SDN) approach to address traditional network architecture limitations, as pointed out by Priyadarsini *et al.* [9].

Data Exchange: These services provide data exchange protocols, enabling operational services to exchange data within SIGRUN (e.g., subscribe messages to the message broker).

VIF Core Services: These services provide the necessary functions to set-up, deploy and orchestrate the VALKYRIES federation. They enable a highly dynamic environment, where deployed services, at any time, can operate in a secure environment, enter or leave the federation, discover services and exchange data without the need to know the topology of the services in use. The VIF core services encompass the following services:

- The **Single Sign-On service & User registration** (SSO) provides authentication in the VALKYRIES system, functioning across the federation's different applications and services. It also supports registration of users and definition of roles within the federation. The SSO is a centralised service in VALKYRIES.
- The **Registration service** provides the mechanisms to register applications and components in the VALKYRIES system, thus becoming known in the federation. This service is a centralised service in VALKYRIES.
- The **SIGRUN time service** provides the reference time to the VALKYRIES system and thus consequently to VALKYRIES's applications and services. This service is a centralised service in VALKYRIES.
- The **Message broker service**, which can be realised by a single server or a cluster of servers, allows applications to exchange data following the publish-subscribe mechanism. The mechanism supports event-based processing by notifying subscribers when new messages are published.
- **Blockchain (BLC) based services** tracks exchanged data in VALKYRIES and stores the metadata and the transactional data in the BLC network. The BLC services function as a secure trace and auditing mechanism in VALKYRIES.

IV. VALKYRIES DATA MODEL AND METADATA

VALKYRIES defines data models representing MCI and emergency response information. The data models are designed to be agnostic of data producers' characteristics, being well adapted to support different types of producers, which can be sensors, algorithms and human inputs. The data model defines MCI specific data, represented by a MDS and associated metadata, as introduced next.

A. *Minimum Data Set*

A MDS is a structured collection of data associated with a unique body of work. It is designed to represent MCI-related information in SIGRUN, including the necessary information to support a coordinated action of the federated organisation. The MDS is structured into six main categories, as presented in Table III.

TABLE III. MINIMUM DATA SET CATEGORIES

Category	Description
Incident Data	Data related with an MCI. It observes EDXL and EIDO specifications.
Vehicle Data	Data concerning vehicles used in an MCI, like ambulances. It observes FHIR and EIDO specifications.
Smart Devices and IoT Data	Data related with connected devices and IoT, such as victims' vitals, fire detection and air quality. It observes FHIR and SAREF specifications.
First Responders Data	Data related to first responders. It observes EIDO and FHIR specifications.
Victim Data	Information collected about a victim during an MCI. This includes triage information, location and injuries. It observes FHIR standards.
Hospital Incident Data	Information about a hospital capabilities and capacity in receiving and treating victims. It observes EDXL, EDXL-HAVE and FHIR standards.

B. Metadata

Every generated message in VALKYRIES contains associated metadata, providing mechanisms to trace, control and restrict how it is handled and shared. The metadata includes:

- Timestamp: date and time the message was generated.
- ProducerID: identifier of the artifact (e.g., sensor or application) that generated the data.
- DataTimeValidity: time validity of the information.
- OwnerID: identifier of the owner of the data, used for traceability purposes and assure compliance with the General Data Protection Regulation (GDPR) [10].
- PriorityLevel: priority of the message.
- UserID: identification of the user that generated the data;
- Shared: flag indicating if the data is authorised to be shared cross-border.

VALKYRIES functions as a cooperative environment allowing entities to exchange data. Since the environment involves sensitive data, VALKYRIES implements mechanisms to trace and audit messages, as well as information flows. VALKYRIES stores all metadata in a Blockchain service, ensuring immutability and security. Blockchain auditing tools can be used, for example, in case a post-event assessment is needed.

V. CONCLUSION

This paper presents the work performed in the VALKYRIES project towards defining a technical architecture capable of enabling collaboration among multiple agencies operating in a cross-border MCI. The definition of the VALKYRIES architecture considers actors, artifacts and information flows involved in a cross-border MCI, from which an interoperability framework, named VIF, was defined. Organisations complying with VIF are empowered to easily participate in a federated collaborative environment, exchange MCI-related information and achieve high-levels of shared situational awareness, thus contributing towards a better employment of resources and improving the mission's effectiveness and efficiency. Next steps of VALKYRIES will involve to further detail the technical architecture and to validate its operational performance in several realistic demonstration scenarios planned for 2023 in Portugal, Spain, Bulgaria, Slovakia, Italy, Greece and Norway, as part of the VALKYRIES Action. A key objective will be to develop technical specifications serving as the basis for a standard, thus benefitting all organisations involved in MCI and cross-border emergency situations.

ACKNOWLEDGMENT

Funding: "This research has received funding from the European Union´s Horizon 2020 research and innovation programme under grant agreement: N° 101020676". The authors would like to thank all the partners of the VALKYRIES Action that supported and contributed to the concepts developed.

The authors declare no conflict of interest.

REFERENCES

[1] VALKYRIES website. https://www.valkyries-h2020.eu. [Retrieved: February, 2023].

[2] OASIS. 2013. *Emergency Data Exchange Language (EDXL)* Distribution Element Version 2.0. Available at: https://docs.oasis-open.org/emergency/edxl-de/v2.0/cs02/edxl-de-v2.0-cs02.html. Dated: September, 2013. [Retrieved: February, 2023].

[3] NENA. 2022. *NENA Standard for Emergency Incident Data Object (EIDO)*. NENA-STA-021.1-2021. Dated: October 19, 2021. Approved: April 4, 2022. [Retrieved: February, 2023].

[4] FHIR Website. https://www.hl7.org/fhir/. Accessed version 4.3.0 generated at 2022-May-28. [Retrieved: February, 2023].

[5] ETSI. 2020. *SmartM2M; Smart Applications; Reference Ontology and oneM2M Mapping*. ETSI TS 103 264 V3.1.1 (2020-02). [Retrieved: February, 2023].

[6] Fielding, R., *Architectural Styles and the Design of Network-based Software Architectures*". Doctoral Dissertation, University of California, Irvine, Sep-tember 2000. Available at: http://roy.gbiv.com/pubs/dissertation/top.htm. [Retrieved: February, 2023].

[7] OASIS. 2019. *MQTT Version 5.0. OASIS Standard*. Available at: https://docs.oasis-open.org/mqtt/mqtt/v5.0/mqtt-v5.0.html. [Retrieved: February, 2023].

[8] W3C. 2021. *WebRTC 1.0: Real-Time Communication Between Browsers*. W3C Recommendation. Dated: 26 January 2021. Available at: https://www.w3.org/TR/webrtc/. [Retrieved: February, 2023].

[9] Priyadarsini, M., and Bera, P., *Software defined networking architecture, traffic management, security, and placement: A survey*. Computer Networks, 192, 2021.

[10] Regulation (EU) 2016/679 of The European Parliament and of The Council. Of 27 April 2016. Available at: https://eur-lex.europa.eu/legal-content/EN/TXT/?uri=CELEX%3A02016R0679-20160504

Rapid and Accurate Time Synchronization using Visible Light for Mobile Sensing

Masanori Sugimoto
School of Information Science and Technology, Hokkaido University
Sapporo, Japan, sugi@ist.hokudai.ac.jp

***Abstract*—A novel time-synchronization technique for mobile sensing is proposed. It uses an LED source to transmit a multiplexed linear-chirp optical signal and a rolling-shutter camera to capture a reflected image illuminated by the signal. The proposed technique can estimate the time difference between the start time of the transmitted signal and the shutter release time of the camera both accurately and robustly. Experimental results demonstrated that the technique can achieve time difference estimation errors of 8.075 $\times 10^{-8}$ s at the 90th percentile for a single image.**

***Index Terms*—time synchronization, multiplexed chirp signal, rolling-shutter camera**

I. Introduction

Highly functional and inexpensive image-sensing devices have become available recently, and collecting sensing data from the real world has become much easier, which is accelerating many developments in our data-centered society. For example, the vast and rapid penetration of smartphones with multiple embedded sensors is enabling the seamless data capture of users' daily activity data, which is driving the development of a variety of applications for personal use, such as activity recording and health monitoring. The data collected can also be used for supporting communities through infrastructure applications such as smart cities and smart government [1].

In sensing technologies, spatiotemporal information (i.e., where and when the data is captured) is critical for time-series data analyses that rely on accurate timestamps and must link with contextual and situational information based on accurate localization. For positioning techniques that estimate distance via the propagation time of wireless signals, their performance is affected by the accuracy of time synchronization between transmitters and receivers. The Network Time Protocol (NTP) [2] and the Precision Time Protocol (PTP) [3] which are standard time synchronization techniques for distributed systems on the Internet, and the Flooding Time Synchronization Protocol (FTSP) [4] which is well-known in wireless sensor network communities and its extensions have so far been proposed. These techniques conduct multiple packet exchanges between nodes and may need between several seconds and hours to achieve the required time-synchronization performance. Therefore, they do not always satisfy the demands for real-time systems in dynamic environments.

In this paper, time-synchronization techniques are defined as techniques for estimating time differences between multiple distributed nodes that each have their own clock. The proposed time-synchronization technique in this paper uses an LED source installed in an indoor environment and a rolling-shutter camera. A modulated optical signal transmitted from the LED illuminates a reflector and the reflected image is photographed by a rolling-shutter camera. The line sensor number having the minimum intensity value is identified from this captured image. By using this number, the time difference between the starting time of the transmitted signal from the LED source and the shutter release timing for this line sensor in the camera can be calculated and used for accurate time synchronization between LED source and camera. A multiplexed linear-chirp signal composed of multiple chirp signals with different sweep frequency bandwidths has been designed using a mathematical model of a rolling-shutter camera working as a frequency filter. As the line sensor number having the minimum intensity converges to the same value when it is detected using chirp signals with different sweep frequency bandwidths, it is possible to achieve accurate and robust time difference estimation.

Experiments to investigate the performance of the proposed technique were conducted to evaluate its performance under a variety of conditions. The experimental parameters varied included the exposure time ratio of the camera, the sweep frequency bandwidth of the multiplexed linear-chirp signal, the distance between the camera and reflector, the type of reflector and the illumination conditions.

The contributions of the paper are summarized as follows.

- A novel time-synchronization technique using an LED source and a rolling-shutter camera is proposed. Multiplexed linear-chirp signals were designed by following the mathematical model of a rolling-shutter camera derived by the author's group [5]. The line sensor number (identified by the minimum intensity of a photographed reflected image) is shown to be represented by a linear relationship involving the exposure time ratio of the camera, the starting time of the transmitted signal, and the shutter release timing of the camera. It is independent of the sweep frequency bandwidths of the constituting chirp signals. By using this linear equation, accurate and robust time difference estimations are available.
- The proposed technique was implemented and evaluated through experiments in real environments. It was found that the technique could achieve time difference estimation errors of 8.075×10^{-8} s at the 90th percentile, using a single image captured from a white paper reflector placed

0.5 m away from the camera with no ambient lighting.

The paper is organized as follows: Section II summarizes previous work related to time-synchronization techniques. Section III describes the details of the proposed technique, including its theoretical aspects and design issues regarding the transmitted signals. Section IV gives the experimental results for the performance evaluation of the proposed technique. Findings indicated through the experimental results are discussed in Section V. Section VI concludes the paper.

II. Related Work

Many existing time-synchronization techniques and systems use wired or radio-wave communications. These time-synchronization studies are included in this overview to help explain relationships within the proposed technique, although they are implemented in different ways from those using optical signals.

Time-synchronization techniques have been investigated throughout the field of distributed systems. The main problems in realizing time synchronization between multiple nodes are the estimation of the time offset for finding an accurate timestamp, measuring time delays in sending and receiving messages, and detecting clock skew. The NTP [2] and PTP [3] protocols are used to time-synchronize servers and clients on the Internet to achieve submillisecond and submicrosecond accuracy, respectively. However, it takes from tens of seconds to several hours to achieve their target accuracy.

Many methods for WSNs have been proposed. In Reference-Broadcast Synchronization (RBS) [6], neighboring nodes that receive a reference broadcast compare the arrival times according to their local clocks to estimate their time offset and clock skew. One problem with RBS is that the comparison requires many message exchanges ($(N+1)/2$ for N nodes). In delay-measurement time synchronization [7], a one-time broadcast from a master node allows slave nodes to time synchronize by estimating the time delay at each slave node. In the timing-sync protocol for sensor networks [8], a root node works as a master clock node and extends a hierarchical structure by exchanging timestamps between a parent and its child nodes to identify the clock drift and propagation delay between them. FTPS [4] sends periodical flooding messages from a master node. A slave node conducts regression calculations by employing multiple pairs of global timestamps from the master node and its own local timestamps. Glossy [9] implements a time-synchronization technique similar to that of FTPS. To achieve successful message decoding without capture effects, it sets periodical time slots for message flooding that are exclusively separated from other application tasks executed on each node. In FTPS, clock skews between master and local nodes increase exponentially with the number of nodes. PulseSync [10] alleviates this problem and has been demonstrated as reducing the clock skews to the order of the square root of the number of nodes. The time-of-flight aware time-synchronization protocol [11] achieves submicrosecond accuracy over 22 hops by conducting propagation delay compensation. CESP [12] was proposed as a method for estimating time offset and drift between master and slave nodes, by receiving packets from reference nodes to reduce communication overhead and energy consumption. Shi et al. [13] extended FTSP from one-way to two-way message exchange with maximum-likelihood estimation to generate time skew/offset compensation. A problem with average-consensus-based time-synchronization algorithms [14] is longer convergence time required to achieve a common value among nodes, caused by the many iterative message exchanges between them. MACTS [15] generates virtual connections between multihop nodes, aiming to reduce this convergence time.

Zhong et al. [16] proposed On-Demand Time Synchronization (ODS), which can adjust clock calibration intervals for desired levels of accuracy. After the demand for a particular offset estimation error is set, ODS adjusts its parameters to satisfy the demand with a given confidence probability. Virtual high-resolution time [17] used high-speed and low-speed clocks to achieve high-resolution time synchronization with low power consumption by coordinating the use of the two clocks. Time delays, including timestamps when sending and receiving messages, are modeled as exponential random variables. To achieve time synchronization in a computationally efficient manner, a low-complexity maximum-likelihood estimator has been proposed [18]. A general model for estimating clock skew and time offsets using the Kalman Filter method has also been developed [19].

Radio-wave-based techniques that run on WSNs [4], [9]–[11] can achieve submicrosecond synchronization but have to be implemented using real-time operating systems, which are yet to be adopted for current smartphones and tablet PCs. This limitation makes it much more difficult to obtain accurate and precise timestamps using commercially off-the-shelf (COTS) mobile devices than it is using WSNs. When a target application implements indoor positioning in mobile settings, it is desirable to complete the time synchronization as rapidly as possible. Radio-wave-based techniques conduct repeated message exchanges between nodes to estimate their timestamps accurately, but such frequent message exchanges may induce traffic congestion or require long synchronization times (several seconds to tens of minutes).

In an alternative approach, an ultrasound time-synchronization technique has been proposed [20]. By calculating the location of the smartphone using time-difference-of-arrival trilateration, the time offset for sending a signal from the speakers time-synchronized with a master clock can be estimated. If a microphone array using multiple smartphones is used to estimate the direction of arrival of sounds, all microphones in the array must be time-synchronized. Dia [21] adopted two-level synchronization, whereby synchronization between one master smartphone and the other smartphones, together with synchronization between the CPU clock and the audio I/O clock in each smartphone, was conducted using a least-squares regression method. BeepBeep [22] conducted acoustic ranging for a pair of smartphones by estimating the signal propagation time between the smartphones. Studies such as this do not clearly state how long the synchronization takes, but completing it rapidly would appear to be difficult. One example [21] conducts regression calculations using multiple timestamp data obtained through message exchanges and others [20], [22] employ specific time intervals between the signal emissions from each smartphone to avoid reverberations, thereby making rapid synchronization difficult.

Regarding time-synchronization techniques using optical signals, FLIGHT [23] was implemented using a fluorescent lamp and the 10-kHz-sampling built-in light sensor on a WSN sensor node called TelosB. The stable nature of the alternating-current frequency enabled time synchronization within tens of microseconds. Alternatively [24] uses a single LED that can be used for transmitting and receiving optical signals. When the LED is switched to receiver mode, it can be used to measure the differences in the charged voltages between two time slots to achieve time synchronization.

Some techniques using a camera have been proposed for illumination-based time synchronization. PSync [25] used an LED illumination source as a transmitter of De Bruijn sequences and a photo detector as a receiver for rapid and energy-efficient time synchronization. Akiyama et al. [26] and Sugimoto et al. [5] proposed techniques using a camera to capture modulated optical signals emitted from LED sources for acoustic localization. To achieve rapid execution of an algorithm based on a phase-locked loop, use of a high-speed (1,000 fps) camera has been proposed [27]. SocialSync [28] can time synchronize multiple smartphones for 3D construction and scene-depth estimation. This technique can estimate the delay between a camera I/O event and a timestamp given by the application software to receive an image frame with millisecond accuracy.

Our proposed technique can be implemented using COTS mobile devices without any additional hardware, and its rapid time synchronization can be achieved with submicrosecond accuracy, which is not possible with existing camera-based systems or techniques.

III. Proposed Technique

This section describes issues regarding the proposed technique.

A. Mathematical Model of a Rolling-shutter Camera

Aiming for low energy consumption, smartphone built-in cameras implement a rolling-shutter technique, whereby the incoming optical 2D image is treated as an array of scan lines, with the overall image being captured as a sequence of line-by-line scans from each line sensor. A mathematical model of the rolling-shutter camera is briefly described in this section (see [29] for details).

B. Design of the Transmit Signal

Let $s(t)$ denote a periodical optical signal emitted from an LED source and let f_C, $T(=1/f_C)$, η, and L denote the frame rate, frame period, exposure time ratio, and total number of line sensors for a camera, respectively. Here, f_C is regarded

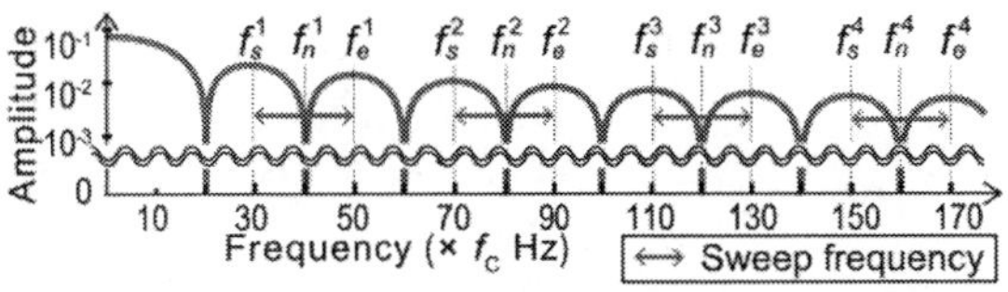

Fig. 1. A rolling-shutter camera as a frequency filter (η=0.05).

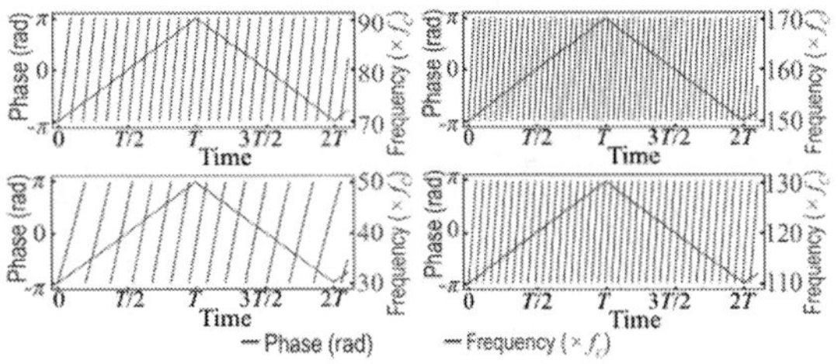

Fig. 2. Frequencies and phases of a multiplexed linear-chirp signal (η=0.05, N_f=4).

as the fundamental frequency of $s(t)$ when the readout time of the line sensors is not considered and δT $(0.0 \le \delta < 1.0)$ is the time difference between the starting time of $s(t)$ and the shutter release time of the first line sensor. The intensity value $r(\tau_l)$ at the l-th line sensor is given by Equation (1).

$$r(\tau_l) = \frac{1}{T}\int_0^{\eta T} s(t + \delta T + \frac{l}{L}T)dt \tag{1}$$

Note that $\tau_l = \delta T + lT/L$ represents the time difference between the starting time of $s(t)$ and shutter release time of the l-th line sensor. Let S_k and $R_k(l)$ $(k = 0, \pm 1, \pm 2, \cdots)$ denote the Fourier transforms of $s(t)$ and $r(\tau_l)$, respectively. The value for $R_k(l)/S_k$, their spectrum ratio, is then given by Equation (2) and is illustrated in Figure 1.

$$\frac{R_k(l)}{S_k} = \eta e^{jk\eta\pi(1+2l/L)}\,\mathrm{sinc}(k\eta\pi) \tag{2}$$

Here, k means the frequency order of the camera frame rate f_C and $\mathrm{sinc}(x)$ is defined as $\mathrm{sinc}(x) = \sin(x)/x$.

1) Multiplexed Linear-chirp Signal and its Characteristics: Figure 1 shows that there are multiple frequencies f_n^i $(i = 1, 2, \cdots)$ for which $R_k(l)/S_k = 0$ (null) holds. From Equation (2), $k\eta = m_i$ (m_i: integer other than zero) is obtained because $\mathrm{sinc}\,(k\eta\pi) = 0$ holds. A multiplexed linear-chirp signal represented by Equation (3) and transmitted from an LED source is composed of a chirp signal whose sweep frequency band is $[f_s^i - f_e^i]$, including $f_n^i = m_i/\eta f_C$, with f_s^i and f_e^i being the nearest spectrum peaks to f_n^i (Figure 1).

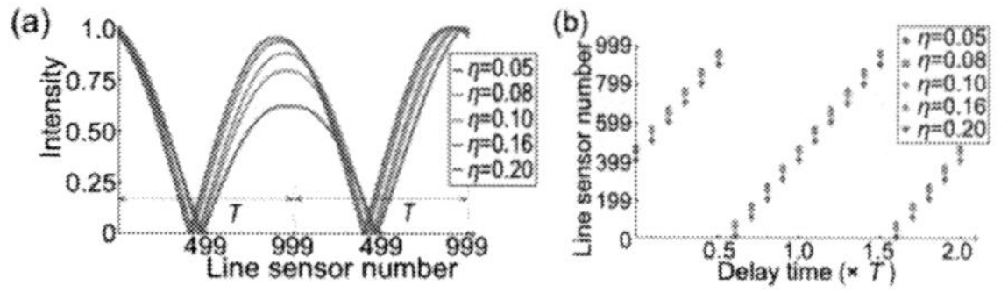

Fig. 3. (a) Intensity values for the range of line sensors (normalized by the peak intensity value at each η setting, L=1,000, δT=0.0) and (b) Relation between δT and l_{min} (L=1,000).

$$s(t) = \begin{cases} \sum_{i=1}^{N_f} \exp\Big[j2\pi\big(\frac{f_e^i + f_s^i}{2T}\ \mathrm{Quotinent}[x,y] + f_s^i\ \mathrm{Mod}[t,2T] \\ \quad + \frac{f_e^i - f_s^i}{2T}\mathrm{Mod}[t,2T]^2\big)\Big],\ (0 \leq \mathrm{Mod}[t,2T] < T) \\ \sum_{i=1}^{N_f} \exp\Big[j2\pi\big(\frac{f_e^i + f_s^i}{2T}\ \mathrm{Quotinent}[x,y] + f_s^i\ (\mathrm{Mod}[t,2T] - T) \\ \quad + \frac{f_e^i - f_s^i}{2T}(\mathrm{Mod}[t,2T] - T)^2\big)\Big],\ (T \leq \mathrm{Mod}[t,2T] < 2T) \end{cases} \tag{3}$$

Here, N_f ($i = 1, 2, \cdots, N_f$), Quotinent$[x, y]$ and Mod$[x, y]$ are the number of chirp signals composing $s(t)$, the integer part of the quotient, and the remainder after dividing dividend x by divisor y, respectively.

The signal $s(t)$ is continuous, with a period of $2T$, and is composed of a pair of up-chirp and down-chirp signals, each lasting T. Because their frequencies and phases change continuously, as shown in Figure 2, the intensity values obtained by the camera (given by Equation (1)) will also change continuously. The line sensor number having the minimum intensity value when receiving either up-chirp or down-chirp signals is denoted l_{min} ($0 \leq l_{min} \leq L-1$) and is the same value in all sweep frequency bands $[f_s^i - f_e^i]$. Figure 3 (a) shows the intensity value for the range of line sensor numbers when δT is set to 0. $l_{min} = \arg\min_l r(\tau_l)$ is obtained by Equation (4).

This was confirmed numerically through computer simulations and preliminary experiments in real environments, because l_{min} is found as a solution to $\partial r(\tau_l)/\partial l = 0$, which includes Fresnel integrals and cannot be solved analytically. The time difference δT is calculated by Equation (5).

$$l_{min} = \mathrm{Mod}\big(0.5(1-\eta) + \delta, 1.0\big)L \tag{4}$$

$$\delta T = \mathrm{Mod}\Big(\frac{\arg\min_l r(\tau_l)}{L} - 0.5(1-\eta), 1.0\Big)T \tag{5}$$

Figure 3 (b) shows the relation between δT and l_{min}, confirming that δT can be estimated by using Equation (5) and l_{min}. The period of $s(t)$ is $2T$ and the values of δ obtained by the proposed technique are found in the range $0.0 \leq \delta < 1.0$. Therefore, δT can be determined as the time difference from the starting time of the up-chirp or down-chirp signal.

The value for l_{min} obtained by the proposed technique does not depend on the sweep frequency bandwidths of the chirp signals. It is therefore possible to estimate the time difference accurately and robustly from a range of l_{min} values for multiple chirp signals with different sweep frequency bandwidths. Accurate estimation is further enhanced by using quadratic function interpolation with the intensity values of l_{min} and those of the neighboring sensors to estimate l_{min} for intermediate points.

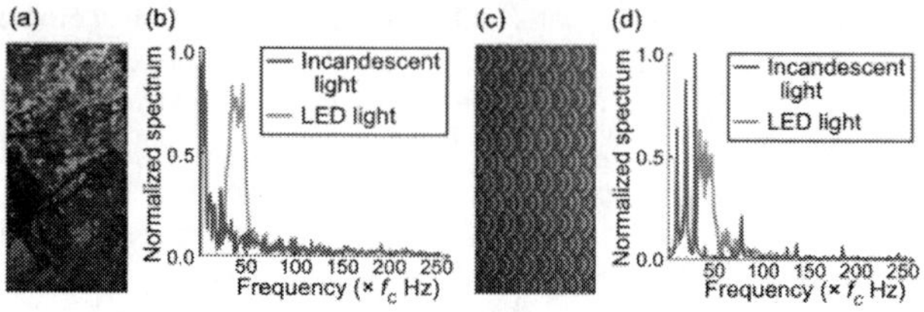

Fig. 4. Reflected images and their spatial frequency spectra: (a) nature image, (b) frequency spectra for image(a), (c) pattern image, and (d) those for image(c).

2) Sweep Frequency: To take full advantage of the features of the rolling-shutter camera, the transmitted optical signal should be received by using all its line sensors. This implies that the transmitted signal should not be captured as direct light from an LED but as an indirect image via a reflector. To determine the sweep frequency bandwidths of transmitted chirp signals, two issues should be considered. First, the frequencies of the signals must exceed the critical fusion frequency to avoid users' perception of flickering [30], and be $L/2\ f_C$ or below because of the sampling theorem. Second, any interference with the spatial frequency spectra of the reflector by the chosen frequency bandwidths of the chirp signals should be attenuated as much as possible.

Figures 4 (a) and 4 (c) show the captured images (exposure time ratio $\eta = 0.10$) of a photograph of red leaves (the "nature image" in (a)) and a traditional Japanese blue-ocean-wave-pattern (the "pattern image" in (c)) illuminated by a chirp signal (sweep frequency in the range $[30.0 f_C - 50.0 f_C]$), which were used as the reflected images. Figures 4 (b) and 4 (d) show the frequency spectra of the images shown in Figures 4 (a) and 4 (c). The distributions of the frequency spectra when illuminated by an incandescent light (the blue line in Figures 4 (b) and 4 (d)) can be approximated to those of the original image because the distribution of the frequency spectra for this light is regarded as uniform. From the figure, note that that the nature image and pattern image both have strong spectra in the low-frequency bandwidths (lower than $30 f_C$ Hz) and the pattern image has strong peaks in the sweep frequency bandwidth $[30.0 f_C - 50.0 f_C]$ and above. Based on this observation, the lowest frequency for the chirp signal was set as $30.0 f_C$ Hz. The influence of the frequency spectra in the high-frequency bandwidths shown for the pattern image is discussed in Sections IV-B3.

C. *Time Difference Estimation Algorithm*

The time difference δT is calculated via the following procedure.

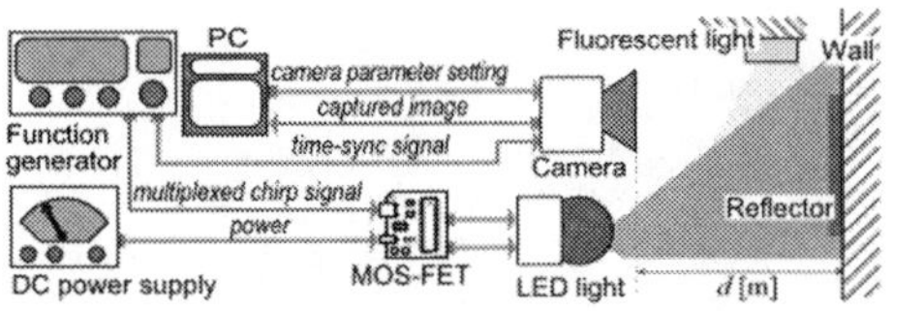

Fig. 5. Experimental environment.

1) The sweep frequency bandwidths for the multiplexed linear-chirp signal are determined from the value of the exposure time ratio η (see Table II for details). That is, $[f_s^i, f_e^i]$ is the narrowest frequency bandwidth including $f_n^i \in [f_s^i, f_e^i]$, where f_s^i and f_e^i denote the peak frequency spectra and f_n^i denotes the null spectrum (see Equation (2) and Figure 1).
2) The multiplexed linear-chirp signal represented by Equation (3) is then transmitted from the LED source.
3) The RGB image $I_{RGB}(i, j)$ $(0 \leq i < M, 0 \leq j < L)$ from the reflector illuminated by the LED source is captured by the rolling-shutter camera ($L \times M$ pixels) and cropped to decrease its size to $L \times M_t$ pixels by selecting a rectangular area determined by $((M - M_t)/2 + 1, 0)$, $((M - M_t)/2 + 1, L)$, $((M + M_t)/2, L)$, and $((M + M_t)/2, 0)$. The RGB image is converted to an intensity image $I_Y(u, v)$ by using the equation $y = 0.299r + 0.587g + 0.114b$, where r, g, and b are the R, G, and B values for the RGB image and y is the intensity value at pixel (u, v) $(0 \leq u < M_t, 0 \leq v < L)$.
4) The mean intensity value for the l-th line sensor i_l is calculated using $i_l = \sum_{u=0}^{M_t-1} I_Y(u, l)$ to obtain the one-dimensional (1D) intensity vector $\mathbf{I} = (i_0, i_1, \cdots, i_{L-1})$. A fast Fourier transform is applied to $\mathbf{I}$ and the spectra of $\mathbf{I}$ are separated into the frequency bandwidth for each chirp signal contributing to the multiplexed linear-chirp signal.
5) The spectra in each frequency bandwidth are converted to their analytic signals. The line sensor number l_{min}, which has the minimum magnitude of the signal, and the magnitudes of its neighboring line sensors are obtained. By applying quadratic function interpolation, intermediate line sensor numbers are calculated. From Equation (5), the time difference δT is found. If the frequency distribution for the reflector is available beforehand, l_{min} can be calculated using only the chirp signals that do not have strong spatial frequency spectra from the reflector in their sweep frequency bandwidths.

IV. EXPERIMENTS

This section shows experimental results of the proposed system.

A. Overview

The experimental environment used to evaluate the proposed technique is shown in Figure 5. The multiplexed linear-chirp signal was generated by a function generator (NF Corporation WF1948), which was connected to an LED source (W-LITE DLFL-001) via a switching power MOS-FET connected to a DC power supply. The purpose of the experiment was to investigate the performance of the proposed method for time difference estimation. The estimation involves the start time of the chirp signal and the shutter release timing of the camera. Being able to release the shutter at an accurate time difference $\delta_{true}T$ and set camera parameters flexibly is critical to the evaluation of the proposed technique, and a high-functional rolling-shutter camera (Point Grey/Teledyne Flir FL3-U3-13S2-C) was therefore used instead of a smartphone's built-in camera. The camera received a trigger signal for shutter release directly from the function generator via its general-purpose I/O interface. The image from the wall-mounted reflector was captured by the camera and transferred via its USB 3.0 interface to a PC, which conducted the calculations described in Section III-C to estimate the time difference δT. The proposed technique was evaluated by comparing δT with $\delta_{true}T$. From inspection of the camera, the maximum exposure time of the line sensors, excluding their readout time, was found to be 8.028 ms for a frame rate of 50 Hz. Therefore, f_C, the fundamental frequency of the transmitted signal in this experiment, was set to $1/8.028 = 124.56$ Hz. The resolution of the camera was 1024×1328 pixels and it exposes two neighboring line sensors simultaneously. The total number of line sensors (L) was therefore $1024/2 = 512$.

As described in Section III-C, the captured image was converted to a 1D vector by averaging the intensity values for the same line sensor. (When many values can be averaged, the noise and the influence of the reflector can be suppressed.) After considering computational complexity and the effects of lens vignetting, a 1024×500-pixel image whose center coincided with the camera optical axis was cropped from the captured image. The sweep frequency bandwidths of the transmitted signals, composed of four pairs of up-chirp and down-chirp for each exposure time ratio η, are given in Table II.

The experimental parameters η, ilc (illumination condition), d (distance between the camera and reflector) and sbj (reflector) were set to a variety of values in five experiments, as shown in Table I. The correct values for the time difference $\delta_{true}T$ (measured using the trigger signal from the function generator) were set as $\delta_{true}T = 0.1 \times i\ T$ $(i = 0, 1, \ldots, 19)$. The time difference estimation was repeated 200 times for each experimental parameter setting, giving 5×3×3×2×20×200 = 360,000 image captures for the experiments.

B. Experimental Results

1) Experiment 1: Exposure time ratio: Figure 6 shows the cumulative distribution function (CDF) values, for each exposure time ratio, of the time difference estimation errors produced using our proposed technique and Figure 7 shows their mean and standard deviation values. Table III shows the 90th percentile errors obtained using single chirp signals for different sweep frequency bandwidths. The best estimation performance results for each exposure time are shown in bold. This experiment demonstrates that the proposed technique can

TABLE I
PARAMETER SETTINGS FOR EACH EXPERIMENT.

Experiment	Exposure time ratio (η)	Illumination condition (ilc)	Distance (d [m])	Reflector (sbj)
Experiment 1	0.01, 0.05, 0.08, 0.16, 0.2	No ambient light	0.5	White paper
Experiment 2	0.01, 0.05, 0.08, 0.16, 0.2	No ambient light	0.5, 1.0	White paper
Experiment 3	0.01, 0.05, 0.08, 0.16, 0.2	No ambient light	0.5	White paper, Nature image, Pattern image
Experiment 4	0.01, 0.05, 0.08, 0.16, 0.2	No ambient light, Fluorescent light, Sunlight	0.5	White paper

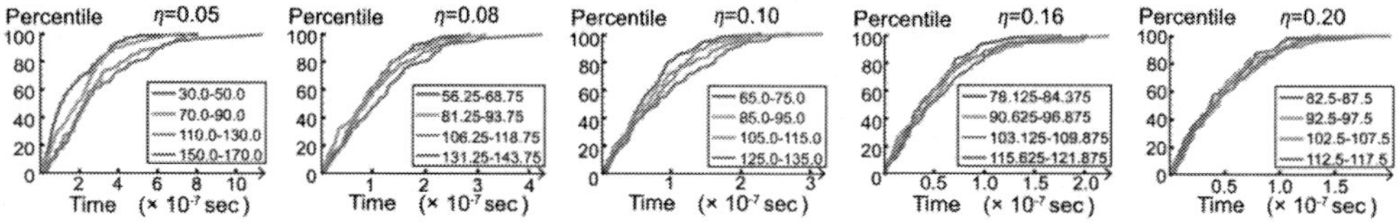

Fig. 6. CDFs of time difference estimation errors for different exposure time ratios.

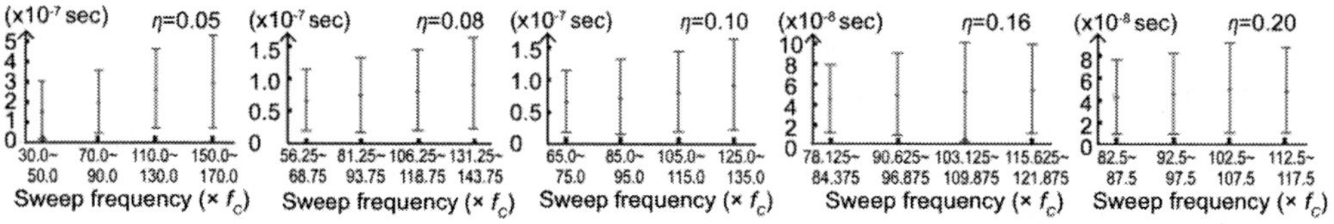

Fig. 7. Means and standard deviations of time difference estimation errors for different exposure time ratios.

TABLE II
SWEEP FREQUENCY BANDWIDTHS $[f_s^i - f_e^i]$ $(\times f_C)$ OF CHIRP SIGNALS FOR DIFFERENT EXPOSURE TIME RATIOS η.

η	$f_s^1 - f_e^1$	$f_s^2 - f_e^2$	$f_s^3 - f_e^3$	$f_s^4 - f_e^4$
0.05	30.0–50.0	70.0–90.0	110.0–130.0	150.0–170.0
0.08	56.25–68.75	81.25–93.75	106.25–118.75	131.25–143.75
0.10	65.0–75.0	85.0–95.0	105.0–115.0	125.0–135.0
0.16	78.125–84.375	90.625–96.875	103.125–109.375	115.625–121.875
0.20	82.5–87.5	92.5–97.5	102.5–107.5	112.5–117.5

TABLE III
90TH PERCENTILE ERRORS FOR DIFFERENT EXPOSURE TIME RATIOS.

Frequency	$\eta = 0.05$	$\eta = 0.08$	$\eta = 0.10$	$\eta = 0.16$	$\eta = 0.20$
$f_s^1 - f_e^1$	**3.336×10⁻⁷**	1.607×10⁻⁷	**1.128×10⁻⁷**	**8.075×10⁻⁸**	**1.012×10⁻⁷**
$f_s^2 - f_e^2$	3.418×10⁻⁷	**1.593×10⁻⁷**	1.322×10⁻⁷	9.285×10⁻⁸	1.112×10⁻⁷
$f_s^3 - f_e^3$	4.791×10⁻⁷	1.898×10⁻⁷	1.544×10⁻⁷	9.650×10⁻⁸	1.273×10⁻⁷
$f_s^4 - f_e^4$	5.623×10⁻⁷	2.157×10⁻⁷	1.753×10⁻⁷	1.035×10⁻⁷	1.164×10⁻⁷

achieve an 8.075×10^{-8} error at the 90th percentile. Significant performance differences for the various sweep frequency bandwidths were not observed, but the best performance was achieved by using the sweep frequency bandwidth $[f_s^1 - f_e^1]$.

2) Experiment 2: Distance: Images from the reflector were captured by the camera for distances of d=0.5 m and d=1.0 m between reflector and camera. The time difference estimation was conducted using the multiplexed linear-chirp signal. The results obtained using the chirp signal for $[f_s^1 - f_e^1]$ are shown in Figures 8 (a) and (b). (Because of page limitations and similarities to the results of Experiment 1, the results for other chirp signal frequencies are not shown.) These two figures show that the 90th percentile errors at the d=1.0 m setting are 1.219 $\times10^{-5}$ s (η=0.05), 2.794 $\times10^{-6}$ s (η=0.08), 2.640 $\times10^{-6}$ s (η=0.10), 2.108 $\times10^{-6}$ s (η=0.16) and 2.383 $\times10^{-6}$ s (η=0.20). Note that the performance deterioration is most significant for the η=0.05 setting than for the other settings.

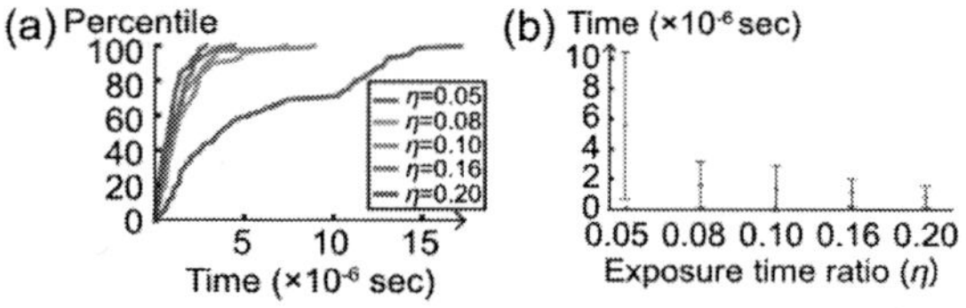

Fig. 8. Time difference estimation errors at the d =1.0 m setting: (a) CDFs and (b) Means and standard deviations

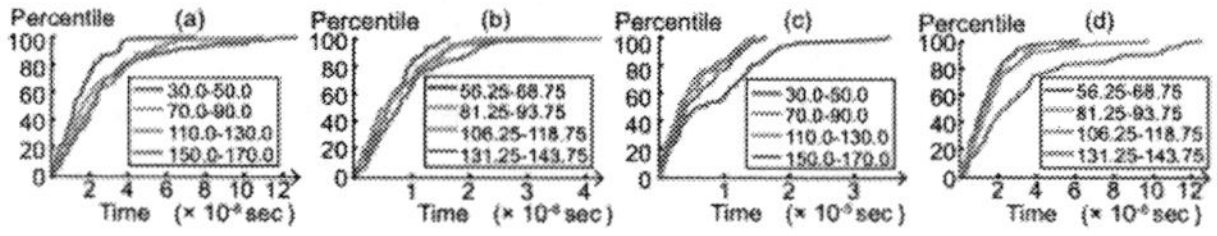

Fig. 9. CDFs using different reflectors: (a) nature image (η=0.05), (b) nature image (η=0.08), (c) pattern image (η=0.05), and (d) pattern image (η=0.08).

3) Experiment 3: Reflector: In Figure 4 (d), note that the pattern image has strong spectra around the 78th and 136th frequency orders of f_C. An experiment was therefore conducted to investigate the influence of the spatial frequencies associated with the reflector. Figures IV-B2 and 10 show the CDFs, means, and standard deviations of the time dif-

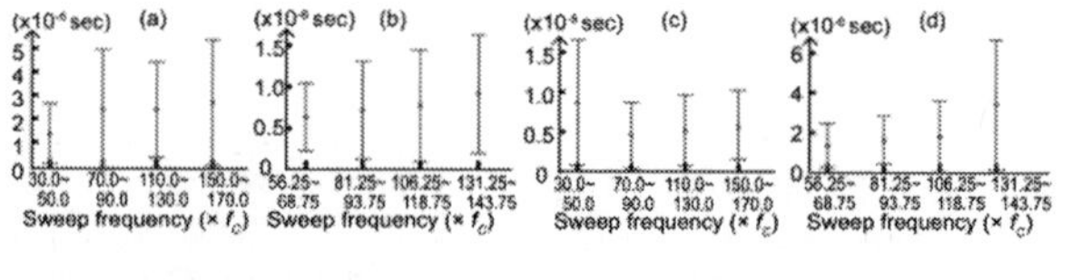

Fig. 10. Means and standard deviations using different reflectors: (a) nature image (η = 0.05), (b) nature image (η=0.08), (c) pattern image (η=0.05), and (d) pattern image (η=0.08).

ference estimation errors by using multiplexed linear-chirp signals (η =0.05 and 0.08) for the sbj="nature image" and sbj="pattern image" settings. The 90th percentile error, mean, and standard deviation obtained by the chirp signal with a sweep frequency $[70.0f_C - 90.0f_C]$ (η=0.05) (including the 78th frequency order) for the sbj="pattern image" settings were 1.808×10^{-5} s, 8.681×10^{-6} s, and 7.836×10^{-6} s, respectively. The results for the chirp signal with a sweep frequency $[131.25f_C - 142.75f_C]$ (η=0.08) (including the 136th frequency order) for the sbj="pattern image" settings were 7.753×10^{-6} s, 3.411×10^{-6} s, and 3.252×10^{-6} s, respectively. From Figures IV-B2 and 10, note the deterioration in time difference estimation performance using a chirp signal with strong spatial frequency spectra from the "pattern image" in its sweep frequency bandwidth. This deterioration is not apparent using a chirp signal with minimal spatial frequency spectra from the "nature image" in its sweep frequency bandwidth.

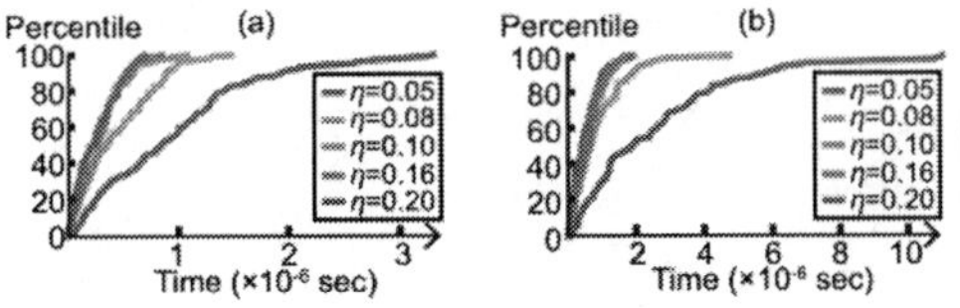

Fig. 11. CDFs of time difference estimation errors for different illuminations conditions: (a) fluorescent light and (b) sunlight.

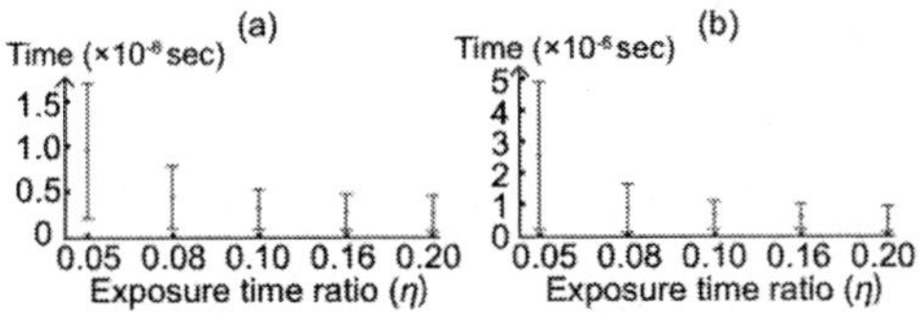

Fig. 12. Means and standard deviations of time difference estimation errors for different illuminations conditions: (a) fluorescent light and (b) sunlight.

4) Experiment 4: Illumination: Experimentation with different illumination settings were conducted and the results obtained by using a chirp signal having the sweep frequency bandwidth $[f_s^1 - f_e^1]$ are shown in the same way as for Experiment 2. Figure 11 demonstrates that the 90th percentile errors for the ilc="Fluorescent light" setting were 1.668×10^{-6} s (η=0.05), 8.525×10^{-7} s (η=0.08), 5.429×10^{-7} s (η=0.10), 4.890×10^{-7} s (η=0.16), and 5.905×10^{-7} s (η=0.20), respectively. The figure also shows that the results for the ilc="Sunlight" setting are 4.676×10^{-6} s (η=0.05), 1.530×10^{-6} s (η=0.08), 1.122×10^{-6} s (η=0.10), 1.044×10^{-6} s (η=0.16), and 1.210×10^{-6} s (η=0.20), respectively. Note that the most significant deterioration is observed for the η=0.05 setting than for the other settings.

V. DISCUSSION

This section discusses findings and limitations regarding the proposed technique.

A. Findings Derived from the Experimental Results

Findings from the experimental results are discussed as follows.

- The results of Experiment 1 imply that the larger the exposure time ratio η, the better the estimation performance of time differences, which is related to the improvement in signal-to-noise (S/N) ratios. Performance differences between the various chirp signals are not significant for the sub="white paper" setting, which does not affect the spectrum distributions in their frequency bandwidths.
- Experiment 2 demonstrates that the 90th percentile errors using the chirp signal having the sweep frequency bandwidth $f_s^1 - f_e^1$ for the d = 1.0 setting are worse than those for the d = 0.5 m setting, as shown in Table IIIand are also related to S/N ratios. Therefore, estimation performance requirements can be optimized by adjusting the power of transmitted signals and/or the distance to the reflector.
- From the results of Experiment 3, performance deterioration is observed when strong spatial frequency spectra associated with the reflector exist in the sweep frequency bandwidths of the chirp signals. If the spectrum distribution of the reflector is known beforehand, it should be possible to retain the estimation performance by selecting chirp signals having appropriate sweep frequency bandwidths and/or by changing exposure time ratios to avoid the spectrum interference. For example, if the reflector shown in Figure 4(b) is used, the estimation performance would best be retained by using chirp signals having sweep frequency bandwidths other than $[f_s^1 - f_e^1]$ ($\eta = 0.05$) or $[f_s^4 - f_e^4]$ ($\eta = 0.08$) and/or by adjusting the exposure time ratio. Figures IV-B2 (c) and IV-B2(d) show that the CDFs using a chirp signal strongly affected by the reflector spectra are clearly different from those less affected. Therefore, if the spectrum distribution of the reflector is unknown, it would be worth investigating the effectiveness of a method that compared the estimation results obtained by individual chirp signals and then eliminating those results that are significantly different from the other results as "outliers" caused by reflectors.
- Experiment 4 demonstrated that the time difference estimation performance deteriorates under the ilc ="Fluorescent light" and "Sunlight" settings, in comparison with that for the ilc ="No ambient light" setting, as shown in Table III. This is caused by their poorer S/N ratios. The estimation results under the ilc ="Sunlight" setting were worse than for ilc = "Fluorescent light" setting, which might again relate to spectral interference with the chirp signals in their various sweep frequency bandwidths. To retain the performance of the proposed technique, therefore, spectrum interference between the transmitted signal and the ambient lighting should be avoided where possible.

B. Limitations

The limitations of this study from a practical point of view can be summarized as follows.

- With many commercially available off-the-shelf cameras, it is not possible to set their camera parameters to arbitrary values, but some setting to predetermined discrete values is allowed. For example, the camera used in this study does not allow setting its exposure time ratio to an arbitrary value. Therefore, it may not be possible to set the camera parameters to the theoretically derived optimum values suggested by Equation (2), which would cause the performance deterioration.

- In the author's previous study [5], it was noted that the camera frame rate may not be stable, with clock drift being observed. Therefore, to retain the performance of the time difference estimation, the frame rate of the camera should be estimated and updated periodically.
- The experimental evaluations were conducted in completely static and stable settings. However, in more realistic situations, the camera and reflector might well be mobile. In future work, the performance of the proposed technique in mobile or unstable environments will be investigated.

VI. Conclusions

A novel time-synchronization technique is proposed in this paper. The proposed technique uses an LED source transmitting multiplexed linear-chirp signals to a reflector and a rolling-shutter camera that photographs the reflected image. It can estimate the time difference between the start time of the transmitted signal and the shutter release time of the camera both accurately and robustly. Our experiments demonstrated that the proposed technique can achieve 8.075×10^{-8}-s time difference estimation errors at the 90th percentile by using a single image captured 0.5 m away from the reflector. Implementing and evaluating the proposed technique using a smartphone's built-in camera are the next steps in this study.

References

[1] R. Khatoun and S. Zeadally, "Smart Cities: Concepts, Architectures, Research Opportunities," *Commun. ACM*, vol. 59, no. 8, pp. 46–57, 2016.

[2] D. L. Mills, "Internet Time Synchronization: The Network Time Protocol," *IEEE Trans. Commun.*, vol. 39, no. 10, pp. 1482–1493, 1991.

[3] IEEE 1588-2019, "IEEE Standard for a Precision Clock Synchronization Protocol for Networked Measurement and Control Systems," `https://standards.ieee.org/ieee/1588/6825/` (retrieved: Oct 6th, 2022), 2020.

[4] M. Maróti, B. Kusy, G. Simon, and A. Lédeczi, "The Flooding Time Synchronization Protocol," in *Proc. of SenSys'04*, Baltimore, MD, 2004, pp. 39–49.

[5] M. Sugimoto, H. Kumaki, T. Akiyama, and H. Hashizume, "Optimally Modulated Illumination for Rapid and Accurate Time Synchronization," *IEEE Trans. Signal Process.*, vol. 65, no. 2, pp. 505–516, 2017.

[6] J. Elson, L. Girod, and D. Estrin, "Fine-grained Network Time Synchronization using Reference Broadcasts," in *Proc. of OSDI'02*, Boston, MA, 2002, pp. 147–156.

[7] S. Ping, "Delay Measurement Time Synchronization for Wireless Sensor Networks," Intel Research Berkeley Lab., Tech. Rep. IRB-TR-03-013, 2003.

[8] S. Ganeriwal, R. Kumar, and M. B. Srivastava, "Timing-sync Protocol for Sensor Networks," in *Proc. of SenSys'03*, Los Angeles, CA, 2003, pp. 138–149.

[9] F. Ferrari, M. Zimmerling, L. Thiele, and O. Saukh, "Efficient Network Flooding and Time Synchronization with Glossy," in *Proc. of IPSN 2011*, Chicago, IL, 2011, pp. 73–84.

[10] C. Lenzen, P. Sommer, and R. P. Wattenhofer, "Optimal Clock Synchronization in Networks," in *Proc. of SenSys'09*, Berkeley, CA, 2009, pp. 225–238.

[11] R. Lim, B. Maag, and L. Thiele, "Time-of-Flight Aware Time Synchronization for Wireless Embedded Systems," in *Proc. of EWSN'16*, Graz, Austria, 2016, pp. 149–158.

[12] F. Gong and M. L. Sichitiu, "CESP: A Low-Power High-Accuracy Time Synchronization Protocol," *IEEE Trans. Vehicular Tech.*, vol. 65, no. 4, pp. 2387–2396, 2016.

[13] F. Shi, S. X. Yang, X. Tuo, L. Ran, and Y. Huang, "A Novel Rapid-Flooding Approach With Real-Time Delay Compensation for Wireless-Sensor Network Time Synchronization," *IEEE Trans. Cybern.*, vol. 52, no. 3, pp. 1415–1428, 2022.

[14] Q. Li and D. Rus, "Global Clock Synchronization in Sensor Networks," *IEEE Transactions on Computers*, vol. 55, no. 2, pp. 214–226, 2006.

[15] F. Shi, X. Tuo, L. Ran, Z. Ren, and S. Yang, "Fast Convergence Time Synchronization in Wireless Sensor Networks Based on Average Consensus," *IEEE Trans. Industr. Inform.*, vol. 16, no. 2, pp. 1120–1129, 2020.

[16] Z. Zhong, P. Chen, and T. He, "On-demand Time Synchronization with Predictable Accuracy," in *Proc. of INFOCOM 2011*, Shanghai, China, 2011, pp. 2480–2488.

[17] T. Schmid, P. Dutta, and M. B. Srivastava, "High-Resolution, Low-Power Time Synchronization an Oxymoron No More," in *Proc. of IPSN 2010*, Stockholm, Sweden, 2010, pp. 151–161.

[18] M. Leng and Y.-C. Wu, "Low-complexity Maximum-likelihood Estimator for Clock Synchronization of Wireless Sensor Nodes under Exponential Delays," *IEEE Trans. Signal Process.*, vol. 59, no. 10, pp. 4860–4870, 2011.

[19] B. R. Hamilton, X. Ma, Q. Zhao, and J. Xu, "ACES: Adaptive Clock Estimation and Synchronization using Kalman Filtering," in *Proc. of MobiCom 2008*, San Francisco, CA, 2008, pp. 152–162.

[20] P. Lazik, N. Rajagopal, B. Sinopoli, and A. Rowe, "Ultrasonic Time Synchronization and Ranging on Smartphones," in *Proc. of RTAS 2015*, Seattle, WA, 2015, pp. 108–118.

[21] S. Sur, T. Wei, and X. Zhang, "Autodirective Audio Capturing Through a Synchronized Smartphone Array," in *Proc. of MobiSys 2014*, Bretton Woods, NH, 2014, pp. 28–41.

[22] C. Peng, G. Shen, and Y. Zhang, "BeepBeep: A High-Accuracy Acoustic-Based System for Ranging and Localization Using COTS Devices," *ACM Trans. Embed. Comput. Syst.*, vol. 11, no. 1, pp. 4:1–4:29, 2012.

[23] Z. Li, W. Chen, C. Li, M. Li, X.-Y. Li, and Y. Liu, "FLIGHT: Clock Calibration and Context Recognition Using Fluoresent Lighting," *IEEE Trans. Mob. Comput.*, vol. 13, no. 7, pp. 1495–1508, 2014.

[24] S. Schmid, G. Corbellini, S. Mangold, and T. R. Gross, "Continuous Synchronization for LED-to-LED Visible Light Communication Networks," in *Proc. of IWOW 2014*, Funchal, Portugal, 2014, pp. 45–49.

[25] X. Guo, M. Mohammad, S. Saha, M. C. Chan, S. Gilbert, and D. Leong, "PSync: Visible light-based time synchronization for Internet of Things (IoT)," in *Proc. of INFOCOM 2016*, San Francisco, CA, 2016, pp. 1–9.

[26] T. Akiyama, M. Nakamura, M. Sugimoto, and H. Hashizume, "SyncSync: Time-of-arrival Based Localization Method Using Light-synchronized Acoustic Waves for Smartphones," in *Proc. of IPIN 2015*, Banff, Canada, 2015, pp. 1–9.

[27] L. Hou, S. Kagami, and K. Hashimoto, "An Advanced Algorithm for Illumination-based Synchronization of High-Speed Vision Sensors in Dynamic Scenes," in *Proc. of ICIRA 2010*, Shanghai, China, 2010, pp. 378–389.

[28] R. Latimer, J. Holloway, A. Veeraraghavan, and S. Ashutosh, "SocialSync: Sub-Frame Synchronization in a Smartphone Camera Network," in *Proc. of ECCV2014 Workshop on Light Fields for Computer Vision*, Zurich, Switzerland, 2014, pp. 561–575.

[29] M. Sugimoto, H. Kumaki, T. Akiyama, and H. Hashizume, "High-Speed Optical Camera Communication Using an Optimally Modulated Signal," in *Proc. of ICASSP 2018*, Calgary, Canada, 2018, pp. 3739–3743.

[30] IEEE Power Electronics Society, "IEEE Recommended Practices for Modulating Current in High-Brightness LEDs for Mitigating Health Risks to Viewers," `https://standards.ieee.org/ieee/1789/4479/` (retrieved: Oct 15th, 2022), 2015.

Easy-to-use Calibration of Inertial Sensors-based Smart Clothing for Consumers

1st Pietro Garofalo
R&D
Turingsense EU Lab
Forlì, Italy
pietro.garofalo@turingsense.com

2nd Michele Raggi
R&D
Turingsense EU Lab
Forlì, Italy
michele.raggi@turingsense.com

3rd Paola Di Florio
R&D
Turingsense EU Lab
Forlì, Italy
paola.diflorio@turingsense.com

4th Carmelo Fiorentino
R&D
Turingsense EU Lab
Forlì, Italy
carmelo.fiorentino@turingsense.com

5th Lorenzo Marchesini
R&D
Turingsense EU Lab
Forlì, Italy
lnz.marchesini@gmail.com

6th Alessandro Montanari
R&D
Turingsense EU Lab
Forlì, Italy
alessandro.montanari@turingsense.com

***Abstract*—Inertial and magnetic sensors are nowadays available as integrated components in common portable devices (smartphones and smartwatches). Despite the continuous reduction of cost and size, their application to the body kinematics is not quite widespread in the consumer market. The main obstacles are the system calibration and setup, in terms of time and complexity. Magnetometers are hard to handle in indoor applications due to inconsistent magnetic disturbances; and the calibration of multiple units can be challenging for non technicians. In order to overcome those limitations, we developed a fast custom magnetometer-free calibration easily reproducible by non technician, to be used in our novel smart clothes [1] (the electronics is fully integrated in the clothes), for applications targeting the consumer market.**

***Index Terms*—Motion Capture, Low-cost MEMS-IMU, 3D Body Kinematics, Biomechanics, Magnetometer-free, Consumer Electronics, Metaverse.**

I. Introduction

Real time human motion tracking has a wide potential in many application fields, e.g., tele-rehabilitation, sport performance assessment, ergonomics [2]-[5]. The gold standard for 3D motion capture (MoCap) is the marker-based optical tracking system. However, those systems can only be used in laboratories with specialized technician, after a time-consuming set-up. These are the reasons why inertial sensors-based motion capture has gained huge popularity in the last few years. In particular, triaxial gyroscopes and accelerometers based on Micro-Electro-Mechanical Systems (MEMSs) are often integrated together to form Inertial Measurement Units (IMUs); if magnetic sensors are included, they are called Magnetic Inertial Measurement Units (MIMUs). MEMS IMUs are cheap, small, self-contained, light weight and easy to be worn. The orientation of the body segments (and thus the joint kinematics) can be estimated by putting those sensors on the body segments of interest. Sensor fusion (SF) and segment to sensor (STS) calibration are crucial phases that strongly affect the overall system outcome [8]-[9]. Through SF algorithms the IMU orientation is estimated by fusing the angular velocity, acceleration and the magnetic field. However, the magnetic disturbances, especially indoor, can lead to inaccuracy; besides, to properly calibrate multiple magnetometers might be too challenging for non-technicians. For what concerns the STS calibration, there is the need for a compromise between the accuracy and the usability by non-technicians. To find this compromise, we developed a magnetometer-free calibration of our smart clothes (shirt and pants with STMicroelectronics inertial sensors integrated, [1]) that can be used at home by non-technicians, once provided with a few instructions.

II. Turingsense Calibration

Turingsense smart clothes (Fig. 1) contain 16 STMicroelectronics LSM6DSR inertial measurement units (triaxial accelerometers and gyroscopes, [8]), are fully washable and come in different sizes. They are chargeable via micro-USB and have fully wireless communication.

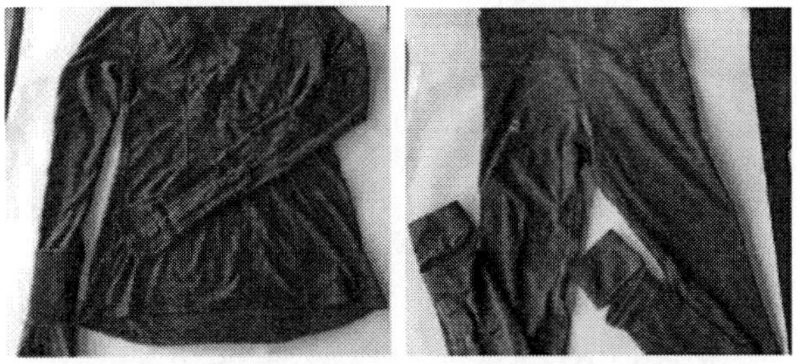

Fig. 1: Turingsense smart clothes [1].

The definitions and the computational procedures needed to obtain the information of the motion of body segments starting from sensor readings (angular velocity and acceleration) are defined as *biomechanical protocol*. In particular, the main objective of the biomechanical protocol is to perform the sensor to segment calibration. The biomechanical protocol used in the Turinsense garment (Fig. 2) has two main steps: (1) N-pose; (2) functional motions [9].

(1) Step 1: N-pose. The first step consists in asking the user to stand still in N-pose (neutral pose). For each IMU, the acquired accelerometer data is averaged to estimate the vertical direction. This averaged accelerometer vector represents an estimate of the anatomical longitudinal direction of the underlying body segment. Moreover, the information from this step is used for the navigation reference frames alignment.

(2) Step 2: Functional motions. The second step consists in asking the user to perform two functional motions: one for the (a) upper body and the other for the (b) lower body.

(a) Upper body: a 90-degrees humeral flexion in the sagittal plane, keeping the elbow and the wrist extended, with neutral elbow pronation.

(b) Lower body: a 90-degrees femoral flexion in the sagittal plane, keeping the knee locked.

During the funcional motions, the recorded gyroscope data is transformed to unit-norm vectors to identify the axis on which the sagittal motion occurs. The average of the normalized gyroscope vectors represents an estimate of the anatomical medio-lateral direction of the body segment where the sensor is attached. [9].

Fig. 2: Turingsense STS calibration.

III. Experimental Results

The Turingsense smart clothes are currently sold in USA and Canada since December 2019. Thus, it is possible to analyze the success rate of the STS calibration among real users. The data stored in the Turingsense cloud database are used for both an inter-subject and intra-subject analyses of the STS success rate at the first try.

The STS success rate among 45 real users is reported in Table I (one trial per user), including single steps and whole procedures rate.

TABLE I: INTER-SUBJECT STS SUCCESS RATE

	N-poses	Arms	Lleg	Rleg	Full procedure
#	37	39	42	42	34
%	82	86	93	93	75

The attemps are detected through specific motion detection algorithms. It is noteworthy that the number of N-poses attempts might include poses where the user had not started to follow the instructions and, thus, not really trying. It explaines the slighlty minor number of successes of the N-pose phase.

In addition, an intra-subject analysis is proposed in Table II, where 8 trials per user have been considered to evaluate the intra-subject success rate of the STS on the first try (i.e. each STS step is performed once).

TABLE II: INTRA-SUBJECT STS SUCCESS RATE

# user	N-pose	Arms	Lleg	Rleg	Full procedure
1	87.5	100	100	100	87.5
2	87.5	87.5	87.5	100	87.5
3	75	62.5	87.5	87.5	50
4	62.5	100	100	100	62.5
5	87.5	87.5	87.5	87.5	87.5
6	100	87.5	100	100	87.5
7	87.5	100	100	100	87.5
8	75	87.5	87.5	87.5	75
9	87.5	100	100	100	87.5
10	87.5	100	100	100	87.5
11	87.5	87.5	100	100	75

IV. Discussion

Results on real user scenarios demonstrate that the calibration steps implemented are easy to perform by non-technicians, and the given instructions allow the user to reach MoCap rapidly. Furthermore, the availability of smart clothing largely simplifies the approach and the acceptability of the user to the technology.

V. Conclusion

The TS inertial system calibration has been developed to be used with TS smart garment, the first consumer clothes with electronics fully integrated. Based on the data, the TS calibration appears to be easy to perform by non-tecnician people, thus highlighting the huge potential to apply this technology to a variety of fields, such as, digital health, fitness tracking, etc.

References

[1] https://pivot.yoga/ Latest access: March 15, 2023.

[2] Truppa, Luigi, et al. "Ballistic skills assessment in semi-professional football players through inertial sensors: the effects of COVID-19 forced rest period", 2021 IEEE International Workshop on Metrology for Industry 4.0 & IoT (MetroInd4.0&IoT), 2021.

[3] Truppa, Luigi, et al. "Assessment of Biomechanical Response to Fatigue through Wearable Sensors in Semi-Professional Football Referees." Sensors, 2021.

[4] Verdini, Federica, et al. "Evaluation of a new wearable technology for kinematic analysis during perturbed posture." 2019 IEEE 23rd International Symposium on Consumer Technologies (ISCT), 2019.

[5] Ligorio, G., et al. "A full-body 3d reconstruction of yoga poses through inertial sensing." Gait & Posture, 2018.

[6] Garofalo, Pietro, et al. "Inter-operator reliability and prediction bands of a novel protocol to measure the coordinated movements of shoulder-girdle and humerus in clinical settings." Medical & biological engineering & computing, 2009.

[7] Raggi, M., et al. "Gait analysis through inertial sensors in transfemoral amputees: Step and stride regularity." Gait & Posture, 2006.

[8] https://www.st.com/en/mems-and-sensors/lsm6dsr.html#overview Latest access: March 15, 2023.

[9] Ligorio, Gabriele, et al. "A wearable magnetometer-free motion capture system: Innovative solutions for real-world applications." IEEE Sensors Journal, 2020.

MRI-Compatible Cascaded Blood Pressure Microsensor

1st Lodewijk Arntzen, *THUAS, Delft, NL*, *l.h.arntzen@hhs.nl*
2nd Daan Boesten, *THUAS, Delft, NL*, *d.boesten@hhs.nl*
3th Urs Wyder, *Fontys*, Eindhoven, NL, *u.wyder@fontys.nl*
4th Jan Bernards, *Fontys*, Eindhoven, NL, *j.bernards@fontys.nl*
5th Paolo Sberna, *TUD, Delft, NL*, *P.M.Sberna@tudelft.nl*
6th Francesco Stallone, *TUD, Delft, NL*, *f.s.stallone@tudelft.nl*
7th Hande Aydogmus, *TUD, Delft, NL*, *h.aydogmus@tudelft.nl*
8th Remco Nieuwland, *Somni B.V., Delft, NL*, *remco.nieuwland@somnisolutions.com*
9th Marinus van der Hoek, *VanderHoek B.V., Vlaardingen, NL*, *mj@vanderhoekphotonics.com*
10th Henk van Zeijl, *TUD*, Delft, NL, *H.W.vanZeijl@tudelft.nl*
11th Jan Schreuder, *CDLeycom, Hengelo, NL*, *j.schreuder@cdleycom.com*
12th Guust van Liere, *Unitron, IJzendijke, NL*, *g.vanliere@unitron-group.com*
13th John Bolte, *THUAS, Delft, NL*, *J.F.B.bolte@hhs.nl*

***Abstract*—For the prevention and diagnosis of cardiovascular diseases, the ability to measure cardiac performance is of great importance. A new type of sensor compatible for catheterization is proposed that can diagnose cardiovascular performance while being immune to Electromagnetic Interference (EMI), as well as compatible with Magnetic Resonance Imaging (MRI), with the ability to expand the number of sensors on a single catheter without additional wires. A prototype consisting of three cascaded pressure sensors on a single optical fiber has been fabricated, allowing measurements of important local medical indicators, such as Fractional Flow Reserve (FFR). The fabricated sensor is able to measure blood pressure with a resolution of 3.6 mmHg at a rate of 2 kHz, with room for improvement. Although further work is needed in the miniaturization and integration of the sensor in a catheter, preliminary measurements show promising results.**

***Index Terms*—cardiovascular diseases; blood pressure sensor; MRI-compatible; optical fiber; catheter.**

I. Introduction

In 2020, in the Netherlands alone, 233,808 reported hospitalizations due to cardiovascular disease were reported [1]. In that same year, a total number of 36,579 people died as a result of cardiovascular disease, representing 22% of the total mortality. For the diagnosis and prevention of cardiovascular disease, measurements of cardiac performance are of considerable importance. To improve diagnostics, accurate and reliable measurements are critical; for example, to determine cardiac output, Pressure-Volume (PV) curves are often measured with piezo-based pressure sensor arrays on a catheter tip. Measuring pressure in arrays allows measurement of other important local medical indicators, such as FFR [2]. These indicators are essential for medical diagnosis, and are currently standard procedure. However, one of the central problems of piezo sensors is that the detection technique is based on electrical signals, which limits precision and reliability due to high static magnetic fields and EMI. Moreover, it is highly desirable that future detection techniques can combine diagnostic capabilities with MRI [4]. This implies that the performance of the sensor must be independent of high magnetic fields, up to 7 Tesla [5]. A different approach was chosen using integrated optics [3] for the development of a new generation of catheter sensors. Furthermore, it is desired that the sensor is suitable for catheters with a diameter of 6 Fr (≈ 2 mm) or less, and a pressure resolution of 1 mmHg or less. The working principle is based on a single optical fiber consisting of multiple Fiber Bragg Gratings (FBG) separated by any adjustable spacing. Combined with an interrogator, the FBGs measure a shift in near-infrared electromagnetic wavelength proportional to the deformations of a Silicon Nitride (Si_3N_4) membrane at varying pressures.

II. Theory

In fluid dynamics, the most simple form of Bernoulli's Law states

$$P + \frac{1}{2}\rho v^2 = \text{Constant}, \quad (1)$$

where P refers to the static pressure, and $\frac{1}{2}\rho v^2$ refers to the dynamic pressure. This equation is easily derived directly from energy conservation. It implies that a cascade of microscaled pressure sensors can be used to trace stenosis in a blood vessels, as visualized in Figure 1. It also implies that such a cascade is suitable for verifying correct positioning of a stent after surgery - since correct stent positioning would directly cause vanishing blood pressure difference over the stenosis. Poisseuille-Hagen law describes the pressure difference over a cylindrical tube of length L, of a fluid in laminar fluid flow

$$\Delta P = \frac{8\mu L Q}{A^2}, \quad (2)$$

where Q refers to the flowrate $[\frac{m^3}{s}]$, A $[m^2]$ the cross-

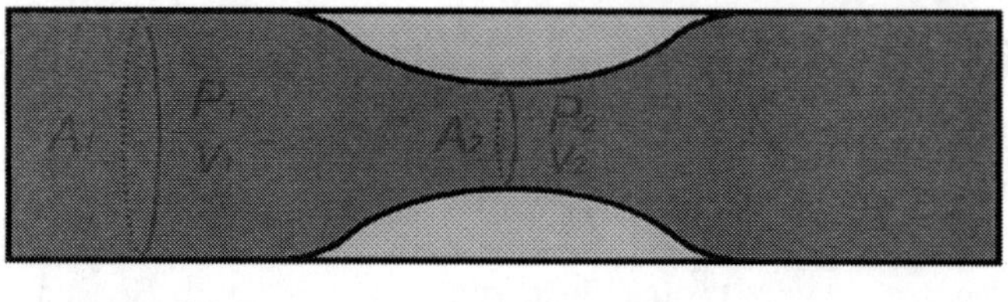

Fig. 1. Bernoulli states a direct relation between cross-sectional areas A_1 and A_2, static pressures P_1 and P_2, and flow speeds v_1 and v_2. If the area reduces, the static pressure reduces, while the dynamic pressure ($\frac{1}{2}\rho v^2$) increases. This implies that a cascaded pressure sensor can be used to trace stenosis in a blood vessel.

sectional area of the cylindrical tube, and μ [Pa · s] the dynamical viscosity. The assumptions in the derivations set some limitations using (1) and (2), but the equations are illustrative for additional applications of a cascaded microscaled pressure sensor. For instance, the proportion of red blood cells in the blood (hematocrit) correlates with the viscosity. An increase of hematocrit leads to a higher viscosity. On average, blood has a viscosity of approximately three times that of water, meaning that the driving pressure to pump blood through the vessels is higher. Polycythemia (or Erythrocytosis) is an anomaly leading to a enlarged hematocrit that can reach up to 70% [7]. The viscosity of the blood will then be up to ten times larger than that of water, making it harder for the heart to pump blood through the vascular system. Equation (2) shows that a cascade of pressure sensors fitted in a catheter show an abnormal pressure decline over the cascade. Additional diagnostic detection is possible, if the sensor cascade has sufficient dynamical response. In that case, it will be possible to analyze the arterial pulse in the time domain, revealing the performance of the heart and vessels [8]. A typical example of a study performed exploring pressure curves with a high precision, is shown in Figure 2. This example shows that analysing the exact shape of the pressure wave can be used as a diagnostic tool.

III. Finite Element Modeling

To verify the feasibility of the sensor, a simulation of the Si_3N_4 membrane was performed using a Finite Element Method (FEM) analysis. In this simulation, the behavior of membranes with thicknesses ranging from 200 to 400 nm was studied under different loading conditions. Calculated deformations of the membranes varied typically from 1.5 to 2.5 micrometers at pressures from 50 mmHg to 200 mmHg, respectively. Given the strain sensitivity of optical fibers with low bend loss, these values are within the measurement range of commonly available optical fibers and interrogators [10] [9]. The FEM model and resulting deformation at a pressure of 200 mmHg is shown in Figure 3.

Fig. 2. Typical example of pressure time domain analysis. Analysing the exact shape and properties, can be used as an diagnostic tool. Adapted from: [8].

IV. Fabrication

The fabrication of the sensor device consists of the fabrication of the Si_3N_4 membrane using photolithographic processes and the adhesion of the FBG to the Si_3N_4 membrane.

A. *Microfabrication of the Silicon Nitride Membrane*

For the microfabrication of the Si_3N_4 membrane, a 300 µm double side polished p-type (boron) Silicon wafer with a <100> orientation is used. Using Low Pressure Chemical Vapour Deposition (LPCVD) with a mixture of NH_3 and H_2SiCl_2, a thin film of Si_3N_4 is deposited on both sides of the substrate. Si_3N_4 was chosen because of its relatively high flexiblity and low etch rate compared to Silicon. The thickness of the deposited Si_3N_4 thin film was measured using an Woollam M-2000 Ellipsometer at a value of 399.47 nm. The stress of the thin film was measured with the use of a Flexus 2320-S thin-film stress measurement instrument at a value of 337.73 MPa. The wafer with a thin film of Si_3N_4 is shown in Figure 4, left.

Using an ASML PAS 5500/60 stepper, rectangular patterns representing the membranes are exposed on a layer of photoresist that is deposited to the backside of the wafer. The exposed patterns are etched away using a Drytek Triode 384T plasma etcher with a mixture of 90% C_2F_6 and 10% Cl_2 until the bare silicon of the wafer remains. The resulting exposed patterns are shown in Figure 4, right. A cavity is created by placing the wafer in a bath of distilled water with 30% potassium hydroxide (KOH) until the silicon is completely etched and only the thin Si_3N_4 layer on the topside of the wafer remains. The silicon wafer with an orientation of <100> etches faster than in the <111> orientation, resulting in a V-shaped cavity with an angle of 54.7 degrees. The cavity, combined with the thin layer of Si_3N_4, acts as a pressure chamber that deforms dependent on the loading conditions. The Si_3N_4 membrane has dimensions of 2.0x0.3 mm. Lastly, the wafer is diced using a diamond saw resulting in rectangular chips with a size of 10x2.5x0.3 mm (LWH).

B. *Adhesion of Silicon Nitride Membrane and FBG*

As shown in Figure 3, the deformation of the Si_3N_4 membrane is the highest in the center of the membrane. Thus, it is

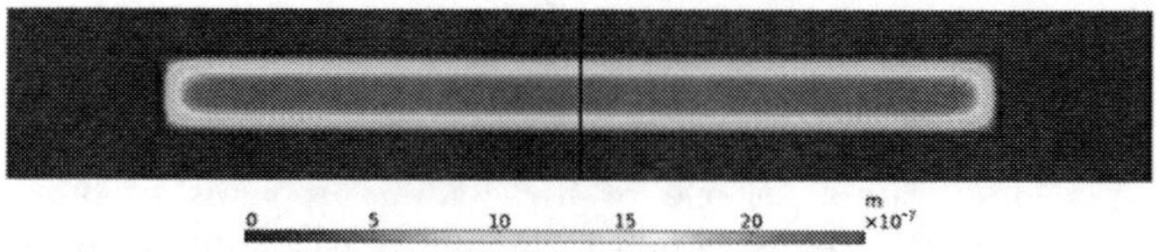

Fig. 3. FEM model of the Si_3N_4 membrane showing the deformation at an applied pressure of 200 mmHg.

Fig. 4. Left: Wafer with a Si_3N_4 thin film. Right: Wafer with exposed patterns representing the membranes.

important to align the FBG precisely at the center of the Si_3N_4 membrane. For this purpose, an alignment setup is made consisting of clamps for the optical fiber, a chip housing and an XYZ micromanipulator with a precision scale of 1.0 µm for the positioning of the optical fiber on top of the membrane. The chip housing is made using an Stereolithography (SLA) 3D printer, and is shown in Figure 5. The aligned optical fiber is bonded to the Si_3N_4 membrane using an UV-curable adhesive with low shrinkage properties [11].

V. Measurement Setup

The chip housing not only holds the rectangular chips with the Si_3N_4 membrane in place, but also has a built-in provision for Luer locks for connecting pressure input and output hoses. The Luer locks allow multiple pressure sensors to be connected together so that pressure changes can be measured simultaneously at multiple points along the optical fiber. The measurement device with three fabricated pressure sensors in cascade is shown in Figure 6. The optical fiber is connected to a FAZT I4G interrogator that measures the wavelength shift of the FBGs at a measurement frequency of 2 kHz with precision of less than 0.1 pm [10]. Blood pressure signals are generated with a Biotek Fluke 601A Blood Pressure System Calibrator that is connected to the measurement device. This device can emulate heart rhythms at different systolic and diastolic blood pressure values.

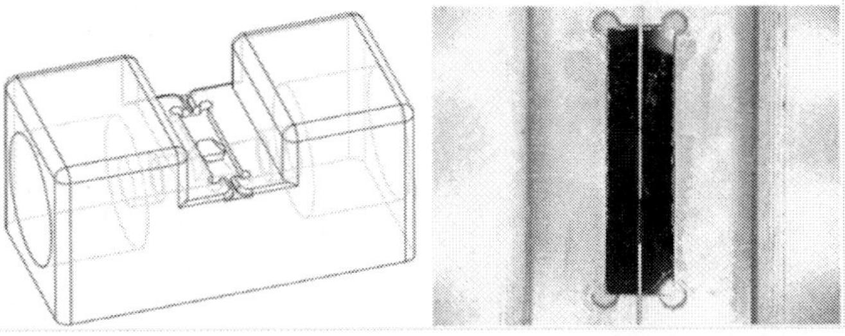

Fig. 5. Left: CAD drawing of the chip housing. Right: 3D printed chip housing with an FBG aligned on top of the Si_3N_4 membrane.

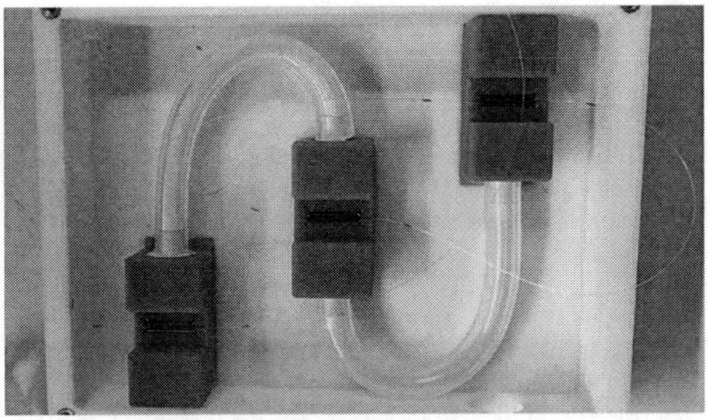

Fig. 6. Measurement device consisting of three cascaded pressure sensors, each on a chip housing, with a single optical fiber.

VI. Performance and Results

The characteristics and performance of the three fabricated blood pressure sensors were determined by applying various loading conditions and measuring the wavelength shift relative to a steady state at 0 mmHg. An Atrial tachycardia heart rhythm at a systolic blood pressure of 140 mmHg and a diastolic blood pressure of 80 mmHg at a frequency of 120 BPM was applied to the measurement device, the result of which is shown in Figure 7. The average wavelength shift of the three sensors is measured at a value of 0.83 $\pm$ 0.05 pm due to a pressure change of 60 mmHg, resulting in a sensor resolution of 3.6 mmHg with the use of an FAZT I4G interrogator. The dynamic response of the sensors is measured at a resolution smaller than 50 ms.

VII. Conclusion

In this study, an MRI-compatible cascaded blood pressure sensor suitable for catheterization was designed, fabricated, and characterized. The dynamic response of the sensors

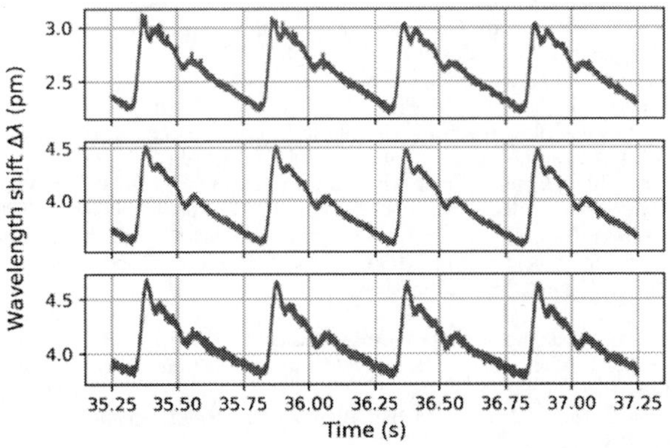

Fig. 7. Performance of the cascaded pressure sensors on a single optical fiber. An Atrial tachycardia heart rhythm was emulated at a systolic blood pressure of 140 mmHg and diastolic blood pressure of 80 mmHg at a frequency of 120 BPM.

was characterized by applying an emulated atrial tachycardia cardiac rhythm at a systolic blood pressure of 140 mmHg and a diastolic blood pressure of 80 mmHg at a frequency of 120 BPM. The dynamic response (measured at smaller than 50 ms) is sufficient to see the specific characteristics in the blood pressure wave. This is an important requirement for determining the suitability of the sensor to measure the performance of the heart and vessels.

The average wavelength shift of the three cascaded sensors is measured at a value of 0.83 ± 0.05 pm shift as a result of a pressure change of 60 mmHg, translating to an average sensor resolution of 3.6 mmHg with the use of an FAZT I4G interrogator. Further work is needed to increase the sensitivity of the sensors to the desired resolution of 1 mmHg. This could be achieved by increasing the deformation of the Si_3N_4 membrane per unit pressure, for example, by increasing the width of the membrane.

To achieve the desired catheter diameter of 6 Fr ($\approx$ 2mm) or less, further miniaturization efforts are required to reduce the size of the chip containing the Si_3N_4 membrane, i.e., by reducing the size of the silicon substrate surrounding the membrane. In addition, future work is planned to the integration of the sensor design into a catheter.

Although preliminary measurements were done to verify the compatibility of the sensors in magnetic fields up to 1.3 T, no measurements have been done yet to verify compatibility with high magnetic fields used in MRI scans. Future measurements are planned to experimentally prove that the fabricated sensor is compatible with the high magnetic fields used in MR imaging.

ACKNOWLEDGMENT

Funding provided by the SIA MKB-RAAK program. We would like thank former Bachelor Physics students Dorus Elstgeest, Lennart van der Hengel, Huib Dijkstra, Nils Boertjes, Lea Visscher, Iris van der Heide and Esther Pot for their dedicated experimental work as well as FEM simulations.

REFERENCES

[1] Hartstichting, "Hart- en vaatziekten in Nederland 2021", pp. 4-27, Dec 2021, https://hartstichting-hartstichting-portal-p01.s3.eu-central-1.amazonaws.com/s3fs-public/2022-11/hart-en-vaatziekten-nederland-cijfers-2021.pdf?, retrieved: Feb 2023

[2] Kathinka Peels, Nico H.J. Pijls, and Bernard de Bruyne. "Measurement of fractional flow reserve to assess the functional severity of coronary-artery stenoses", Jun 1996, publisher: N Engl J Med

[3] Fiber Bragg Grating Strain Sensor Incorporated to Monitor Patient Vital Signs During MRI, 4986, VOL. 13, NO. 12, Dec 2013, publisher: IEEE

[4] Andreas Kumar, David J. Patton, and Matthias G. Friedrich, "The emerging clinical role of cardiovascular magnetic resonance imaging", Jun 2010, publisher: Pulsus Group

[5] UMC Utrecht, "7T-MRI" https://www.umcutrecht.nl/nl/wetenschappelijk-onderzoek/7t-mri, retrieved: Feb 2023.

[6] "Venturi Effect", https://en.wikipedia.org/wiki/Venturi_effect, retrieved: Feb 2023.

[7] John E. Hall, "Guyton and Hall Textbook of Medical Physiology", pp. 155-166, 2003.

[8] O'Rourke, M.F., "Time domain analysis of the arterial pulse in clinical medicine", Med Biol Eng Comput 47, pp. 119–129, Feb 2009, publisher: IFMBE

[9] FBGS, Draw Tower Gratings, Overview, https://fbgs.com/components/draw-tower-gratings-dtgs/, retrieved: Feb 2023.

[10] Femto Sensing International, FAZT I4G INTERROGATOR Datasheet, https://femtosensing.com/wp-content/uploads/2020/01/FSI-FAZ-I4G-Interrogator-Datasheet-V4.pdf, retrieved: Feb 2023.

[11] Norland Products, Norland Optical Adhesive 65 Technical Datasheet, https://www.norlandprod.com/adhesives/NOA%2065.html, retrieved: Feb 2023.

Printed Humidity Sensors And Their Application

Zhiyi Zhang*, Mickey Chen, Salima Alem, Ye Tao*, Ta-Ya Chu, Gaozhi Xiao, Chundra Ramful, Ryan Griffin
Advanced Electronics and Photonics Research Center, National Research Council Canada, Canada
e-mail: zhiy.zhang@nrc-cnrc.gc.ca; ye.tao@nrc-cnrc-gc.ca

Abstract—We have developed a new type of printed capacitive humidity sensors with stacked parallel-plate electrodes. A polymer sensing material with extremely low hysteresis and a grid top electrode design that ensures the sensor's rapid response to humidity changes were used in the sensors. Screen printing, flexo printing and inkjet printing were used to print the sensors with a capacitance value of 400-2730 pF and a sensitivity of 1.2-11.4 pF/%RH obtained, depending on the printing methods. The sensitivity of the printed sensors was found to decrease with a raised temperature, and the temperature effects were attributed to the water sorption in the sensing polymer and its relationship with temperature. A method of calibrating the temperature of the sensors was thus proposed and implemented. With the obtained capacitance value over 400 pF, low-cost electronic circuit PCB boards were designed and fabricated to attach the printed sensors, resulting in standalone and functional humidity sensing units. Each of the humidity sensing units is equipped with light energy harvesting, capacitance measurement, and wireless data transmission, as well as the calibration capability for converting measured capacitance to relative humidity. The units were successfully applied in the building management of commercial office buildings.

Keywords-humidity sensors; printing; filed application.

I. INTRODUCTION

Printing on flexible substrates is an emerging technology for sensor fabrication. With the combination of new solution-based functional materials and cost-effective printing processes, the technology enables large, flexible, stretchable, lightweight devices that were not possible using traditional semiconductor processes [1][2]. Various sensors were fabricated with the technology, and some of them have been commercialized with a great success. Printed glucose sensors alone, for example, already have annual sales of multi-billion US dollars. Many other printed sensors, such as temperature sensors, organic photodetectors, pressure sensors, humidity sensors have either found practical applications or showed promising future.

In our work of applying printed and flexible humidity sensors in high performance building management, we need sensors that have a capacitance value of several hundred pF and can be measured with a low-cost DC circuit. But, the existing printed sensors normally have a capacitance value of several pF and sensitivity in fF/%RH range, and the sensors need a complicated instrument to analyze [3][4]. We therefore proposed parallel-plate structure with a grid top electrode to achieve high capacitance and high sensitivity, and studied the fundamental characteristics and temperature effect of the obtained sensors in detail. With these, we were able to bring the printed humidity sensors to standalone sensing units that can harvest light energy, perform humidity measurement and transmit data wirelessly at regular interval.

In Section 2, experiment details are provided and in Section 3, the results with discussion are presented. In Section 4, the work is concluded.

II. EXPERIMENT

Cellulose acetate butyrate with 12-15 wt% acetyl and 36-40% butyryl content was used as sensing material with ethylene glycol diacetate as its solvent. Silver flake-based ink was used for screen printing electrodes and PET films for substrates. Silver nanoparticles-based ink was used for flexographic printing and inkjet printing. An EKRA X1-SL screen printer, the flexo unit of Testacolor 171 from NSM-AG, and a Dimatix 2800 inkjet printer from Fujifilm Dimatix were used to print the sensors.

The capacitance of the printed sensors was measured with Agilent 4284A LCR meter for dynamic monitoring, and a battery-powered circuitmate capacitance meter (called as DC meter here) from Beckman Industrial co was used in the detailed study of the sensors at various temperatures and under various water vapor pressures. For the packaged sensors, the measurement was done by the PCB boards automatically and periodically. The capacitance-humidity-temperature characterization was carried out in a Burnsco B-Series environmental chamber.

III. RESULTS AND DISCUSSION

In this work, we proposed a new type of printed capacitive humidity sensors with stacked parallel-plate electrodes to achieve a high capacitance value and high sensitivity. Figure 1 shows the structure of the sensor. A solid conductive silver film is first printed on a flexible substrate PET film as the bottom electrode, followed by printing a layer of sensing material to cover the electrode with a large margin. Then, a grid-shaped top electrode is printed on the material. A capacitance value of over 400 pF as shown in Figure 2 was obtained for all the printed sensors when cellulose acetate butyrate is used as the sensing material. No hysteresis effect was observed from the sensors.

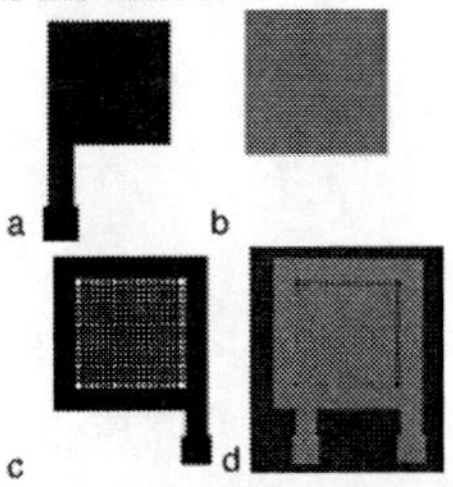

Figure 1. Design of a capacitive humidity sensor and the printed sensor. (a), bottom layer electrode; (b), sensing material layer; (c), top layer electrode; (d), printed sensor.

The sensor performance depends on the thickness of the sensing material (as seen in Table 1), and the achievable film thickness depends on the printing method. Screen printing is only good for printing thick films, and the best sensor performance is 435 pF and 1.2pF/%RH. Flexo printing can print thinner films, 725 pF and 1.8pF/%RH can be achieved. Inkjet printing can very thin films, 2730 pF and 11.4 pF/%RH was achieved. As screen printing is suitable for volume fabrication at low cost, the process was used for printing all the sensors used for study and application.

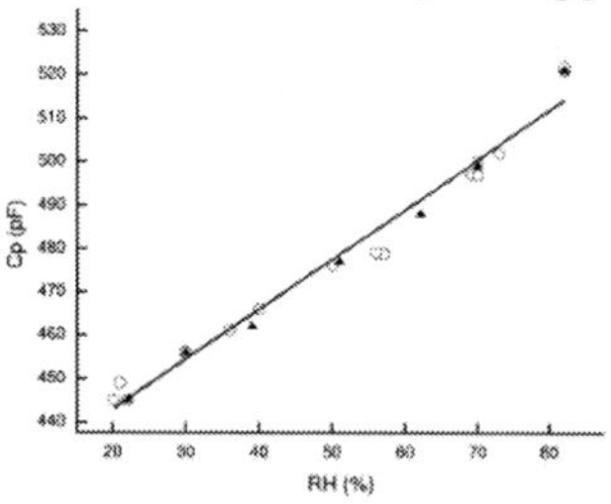

Figure 2. Measured capacitance of a humidity sensor as a function of chamber humidity. (o) measured when humidity was changed ascendingly; (Δ) measured when humidity was changed descendingly.

TABLE 1. EFFECT OF THE SENSING MATERIAL ON SENSOR PERFORMANC

Printing	Thickness µm	Capacitance pF	Sensitivity pF/%RH
Screen printing	18.3	435	1.2
Flexo printing	12.9	527	1.8
Flexo printing	24.8	266	0.6
Inkjet Printing	-	2730	11.4

The performance of the printed humidity sensors was fund related to environment temperature. Figure 3 shows the capacitance-RH plots of a sensor at seven different temperatures. At each of the studied temperatures, the capacitance (Cp) of the sensor responds linearly to the relative humidity (RH) changes. The sensitivity of the sensor - the slope of the Cp-RH plot at each testing temperature was obtained by linearly fitting the corresponding Cp-RH data, and are shown in Figure 4. The sensor sensitivity decreases with increasing temperature, from 1.5 pF/% RH at 5 °C to 1.0 pF/% RH at 45 °C.

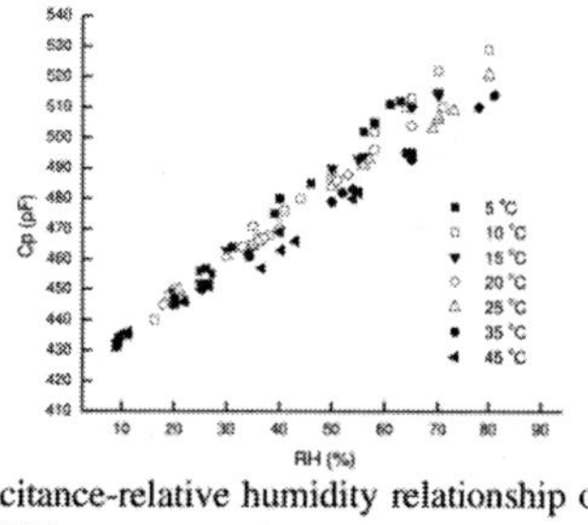

Figure 3. The capacitance-relative humidity relationship of a printed sensor at various temperatures.

The further study at various constant water vapor pressures showed that the capacitance of the sensors decreases with increasing temperature at a constant water vapor pressure, and it increases with increasing water vapor pressure. The reason is that the capacitance change is directly proportional to the water solubility in the sensing material. From the measurement, the sorption of water in the sensing materials was estimated to be from-2.9 KJ/mol to -3.0 KJ/mol.

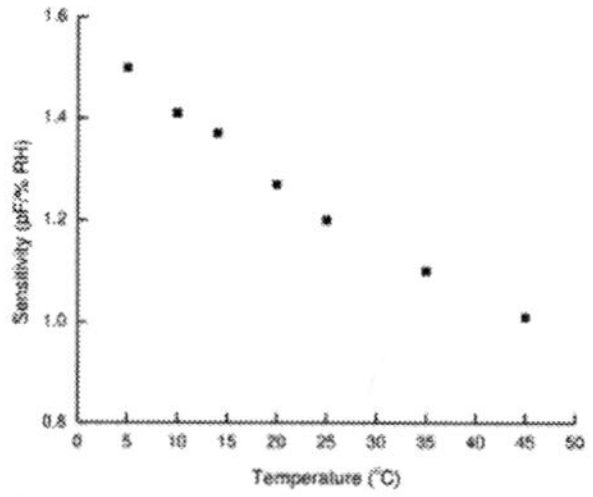

Figure 4. The sensitivity-temperature dependence of a printed relative humidity sensor.

With a capacitance value over 400 pF and a sensitivity above 1 pF/%RH, the printed sensors are acceptable for the measurement with a simple DC circuit in practical field application. A Credit-Sized Printed Circuit Board (PCB) for measuring the sensor's capacitance was thus designed and fabricated for applying the sensors in building management. Figure 5 shows a fully packaged humidity sensor that directly gives humidity reading as a standalone sensing unit. An EnOcean's STM 332U device was incorporated in the PCB for light energy harvesting, data processing and wireless communication. The harvested energy from room light and sun light in day time provides sufficient energy for powering the sensor measurement and data transmission uninterruptedly 24 hours a day. The packaged sensors were successfully deployed in the humidity monitoring and control of an office building. In the application, the sensors were programed to provide humidity data very 5 mins.

Figure 5. A packaged humidity sensor with self-powering and wireless communication capabilities.

IV. CONCLUSION

Printed capacitive humidity sensors with stacked parallel plates were developed to achieve a high capacitance of over 400 pF and a high sensitivity of over 1.0 fF/%RH. By printing a thin layer of the sensing polymer, the capacitance value and sensitivity of the sensors can be substantially increased. It was found that the capacitance reading and sensitivity of the sensors decrease at elevated temperature, due to the intrinsic decrease of water sorption in the sensing polymer. The printed sensors were packaged with simple DC circuits and energy harvesting units as standalone sensing units for practical field application. They were successfully deployed in an office building for dynamic control.

REFERENCE

[1], S. Khan, L. Lorenzelli, and R. S. Dahiya, "Technologies for printing sensors and electronics over large flexible substrates: a review", IEEE Sensors, 15, pp. 3164-3186, 2015.

[2], Y. S. Rim, S. -H. Bae, H. Chen, N. D. Macro, and Y. Yang, "Recent progress in materials and devices toward printable and flexible sensors", Adv. Mater. 28, pp. 4415-4400, 2016.

[3], F. J. Romero, A. Rivadeneyra, A. Salina-Castillo, A. Ohata, D. P. Morales, M. Becherer, and N. Rodriguez, "Design, fabrication and characterization of capacitive humidity sensors based on emerging flexible technologies", Sens. and Actuators B 287, pp. 459-467, 2019.

[4], A. Rivadenenyra, J. Fernadez-Salmeron, M. Agudo-Acemel, J. A. Lopez-Villanueva, L. F. Capitan-Vallvey, A. J. Palma, "Printed electrodes structure as capacitive humidity sensors: a comparison", Sens. and Actuators B 244, pp. 56-65, 2016.

Designing and Manufacturing of Multifunctional Nanosensors Using Ultrafast Laser Processing

Yury V. Ryabchikov
HiLASE Center, Scientific Laser Applications Department
Institute of Physics of the Czech Academy of Sciences
Dolni Brezany, Czech Republic
e-mail: ryabchikov@fzu.cz

Abstract— **Ultrafast laser processing is a well-developed model for the nanostructure synthesis as well as for the material modification. Its employment for sensing applications is a facile route of the development of new types of multi-modal nanosensors with required performance whose efficiency can be improved due to their high chemical purity. In particular, pulsed laser deposition is used for the formation of nanosensors requiring complex synthesis conditions in gaseous atmosphere. In this work, pulsed laser ablation in liquids is employed for the easy synthesis of sensing nanoagents. It allows us to form single- and multi-component (also having semiconductor modalities) nanosensors based on different metallic elements, which are successfully used for biosensing (SERS) and nanothermometry applications.**

Keywords-nanosensors; SERS; nanothermometry; laser ablation; ultrafast laser processing.

I. INTRODUCTION

The development of novel multi-modal nanosensors allowing the detection of changes of various parameters is still an important application task. One of the most perspective scientific directions is the creation of highly-sensitive non-toxic multi-functional bionanosensors able to detect slightest modifications in life organisms. Their design and formation is an important objective for the life science being still very challenging due to various complex issues.

Ultrafast laser processing is a very promising appeoach that is an alternative to many chemical synthesis methods providing the extreme purity of the chemical content of the prepared nanosensors. Here, one can highlight the following approaches for their formation:

1) Pulsed Laser Ablation in Liquids (PLAL) allows direct synthesizing of colloidal solutions of composite nanoparticles merging both semiconductor and metallic elements being a facile route to form nanostructures with variable chemical content [1].

2) Pulsed Laser Deposition (PLD) leads to the deposition of nanostructures on a substrate using a high-vacuum or gaseous environment [2].

3) Laser-Induced Forward Transfer (LIFT) allows transferring of nanoparticles (NPs) on a substrate making patterns with required geometric characteristics.

4) Volumetric Modification (VM) can also be performed by irradiating of a material using a high power laser source with ultrashort pulse duration following by further chemical etchning. Such a technique is used for the design and the formation of microfluidic channels, which are very promising for biosensing applications [3].

Thus, the combination of these techniques by employing only one ultrafast laser source used for the different laser processing lets us the design of novel multi-functional nanosensors. In the current research, multi-element nanostructures were prepared and successfully tested for various sensing applications, in particular, for bioimaging using Surface-Enhanced Raman Scattering (SERS) technique due to the presence of a variable content of plasmonic metals as well as for optical or magnetic resonance nanothermometry that can be promising for cell studies.

II. EXPERIMENTS

To produce multi-element nanostructures, which can be employed for sensing applications, ultrafast laser sources (6 ps pulse duration) with variable laser fluence were used. Colloidal solutions were formed by direct laser ablation of a metallic target immersed in an aqueous solution of various semiconductor (Si, C, SiC, Ge) NPs allowing the combination of different elements in one nanoparticle. The deposition was carried out in a high vacuum by irradiating corresponding metallic or semiconductor targets using the same laser sources. The volumetric modification was performed by the laser irradiation of a substrate at various laser parameters followed by their further chemical etching with the hydrofluoric acid [3]. The formed nanostructures were comprehensively investigated by a set of different methods such as UV-Vis, Raman, Photoluminescence (PL) or Electron Paramagnetic Resonance (EPR) spectroscopies, Transmission or Scanning Electronic Microscopy (TEM or SEM) and X-Ray Diffraction (XRD).

III. RESULTS AND DISCUSSION

The ultrafast laser processing leads to significant changes of processed materials reflecting it by changes of their structural and optical properties. As a base for the design of multi-functional nanosensors, colloidal solutions of such semiconductor nanostructures as carbon and silicon were chosen. This choice was substantiated by their successful applications in bioimaging [4], optical nanothermometry [5], singlet oxygen generation [6][7] or non-linear optical bioimaging [8]. The performed 2-step laser processing considerably modified their properties leading to the appearance of strong plasmonic properties easily controlled by the processing time (Figure 1). Here, semiconductor NPs formed by either laser or chemical methods were successfully used for the design of plasmonic multi-component nanostructures (Figure 1). In the case of C NPs, double-band absorbance was obtained (Figure 1). Besides the achieved plasmonic responses, these nanostructures also revealed strong EPR signals from unpaired electrons due to the presence of certain types of paramagnetic defects [9]. Moreover, X-ray studies of semiconductor-metallic nanocomposites also demonstrated that XRD patterns of semiconductor nanostructures gradually transformed into metallic ones reflecting several crystalline planes corresponded to used for the laser ablation a metallic target.

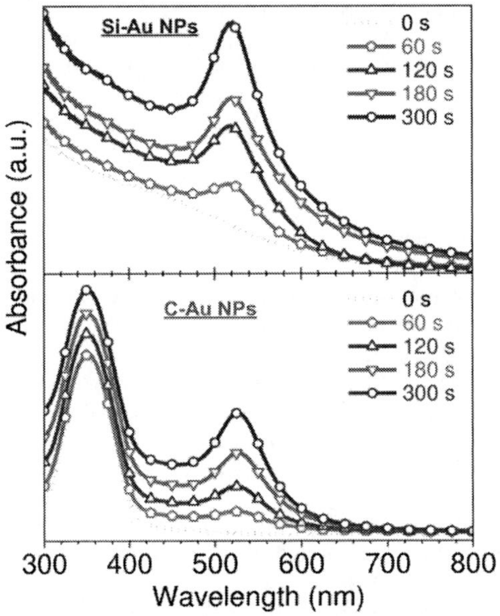

Figure 1. Laser-induced appearance of variable plasmonic sensing modalities in silicon (on the top) and carbon (on the bottom) nanoparticles.

These important modifications opens up a new important niche for semiconductor nanomaterials in the field of nanoplasmonics allowing their implementation in SERS biosensing additionally to the aforementioned applications [10]. Moreover, using the photoluminescence response of semiconductor NPs one can apply them for optical nanothermometry whose efficiency will be significantly affected by embedded noble metal elements acting as either (i) plasmonic resonance enhancers or (ii) metallic quencher of the fluorescence. Furthermore, paramagnetic defects of semiconductor nanostructures can also be employed at the same time as temperature nanosensors for magnetic resonance nanothermometry.

In summary, the design of novel nanosensors based on single- and multi-element nanostructures formed by ultrafast laser processing was demonstrated and their sensing performance was assessed. In particular, PLD technique was used to deposit different plasmonic nanostructures with variable size on a substrate. LIFT technology was employed to design sensors whose performance was considerably influenced by the size and composition of NPs and the distance between them. Moreover, composite NPs with features affected by PLAL conditions were also deposited on a substrate or were used as a concentrated colloidal solution. These nanosensors were used for the detection of (i) bacteria using SERS technique showing 10^5 cfu/mL detection limit for *L.innocua* and *E.Coli* [10], (ii) environment temperature by magnetic or optical nanothermometry showing 0.75 %/°C sensitivity. Thus, such nanosensors can be promising for biosensing, bioimaging and nanothermometry applications.

ACKNOWLEDGMENT

Yu. V. R. acknowledges the funding from The European Union's Horizon 2020 research and innovation programme under the Marie Skłodowska-Curie Actions Individual Fellowship (grant agreement No 897231, LADENTHER); the European Regional Development Fund and the state budget of the Czech Republic (Project No. BIATRI: CZ.02.1.01/0.0/0.0/15_003/0000445) and also thanks Prof. J. Behrends (FU, Berlin, Germany) for the financial and experimental support of the EPR measurements as well as Dr. A. Zaderko (ILM, Lyon, France) for carbon nanodots.

REFERENCES

[1] Yu. V. Ryabchikov, "Facile Laser Synthesis of Multimodal Composite Silicon/Gold Nanoparticles with Variable Chemical Composition", J. Nanopart. Res., vol. 21(4), pp. 85, April 2019.

[2] M. J. Lo Faroa et al., "Surface-enhanced Raman scattering for biosensing platforms:a review", Radiat. Eff. Defect S, vol. 177, pp. 1209–1221, October 2022.

[3] K. Sugioka et al., "Femtosecond laser 3D micromachining: a powerful tool for the fabrication of microfluidic, optofluidic, and electrofluidic devices based on glass", Lab Chip, vol. 14, pp. 3447–3458, June 2014.

[4] A. Kasouni, T. Chatzimitakos, and C. Stalikas, "Bioimaging Applications of Carbon Nanodots: A Review", C, vol. 5, pp. 19, April 2019.

[5] Yu. V. Ryabchikov, S. A. Alekseev, V. Lysenko, G. Bremond, and J–M. Bluet, "Photoluminescence thermometry with alkyl-terminated silicon nanoparticles dispersed in low–polar liquids", Phys. Status Solidi–R, vol. 7(6), pp. 414–417, May 2013.

[6] Yu. V. Ryabchikov et al., "Dependence of the Singlet Oxygen Photosensitization Efficiency on Morphology of Porous Silicon", Phys. Status Solidi A, vol. 204(5), pp. 1271–1275, April 2007.

[7] E. A. Konstantinova et al., "Electron Paramagnetic Resonance and Photoluminescence Study of Si Nanocrystals – Photosensitizers of Singlet Oxygen Molecules", J. Non–Cryst. Solids, vol. 352(9–20), pp. 1156–1159, June 2006.

[8] A. Yu. Kharin et al., "Bi-modal nonlinear optical contrast from Si nanoparticles for cancer theranostics", Adv. Opt. Mater., vol. 7(13), pp. 18011728, April 2019.

[9] Yu. V. Ryabchikov, and J. Behrends, "Expedient Paramagnetic Properties of Surfactant-Free Plasmonic Silicon-Based Nanoparticles", Opt. Quan. Electron., vol. 52, pp. 177, March 2020.

[10] M. Kögler et al., "Bare Laser–Synthesized Au–Based Nanoparticles as Non–Disturbing SERS Probes for Bacteria Identification", J. Biophotonics, vol. 11(7), pp. e201700225, February 2018.

Using a Silicon Drift Detector to Improve an Agricultural Compton Scattering Tomograph for Soil Compaction Analysis

Paulo E. Cruvinel
Embrapa Instrumentation, São Carlos, SP, Brazil
Post-Graduation Program in Computer Science - Federal University of São Carlos, SP, Brazil
Email: paulo.cruvinel@embrapa.br

Abstract— **The use of sensors in farming have become essential for soil, plants and environment monitoring in order to greater yields, while allowing rational use of inputs and decreasing risks. Although many of them are known, still there are challenges related to sensor's development, characterization and customization for agricultural use, bringing opportunities for research and innovation. This article presents a study for the use of a high-performance silicon drift detector in a customized Compton scattering tomograph to analyze soil compaction in agricultural field. In agriculture the soil compaction causes substantial reduction in productivity and has always been of great concern for farmers. The use of such a methodology enables non-invasive and non-destructive measurements of soil compaction directly in the crop area, i.e., allowing its mapping. Energy resolution and signal-to-noise ratio were evaluated and compared with those from a classic scintillation detector. Based on the results, it was concluded that such a sensor can improve the effectiveness of a Compton scattering tomograph dedicated for soil compaction measurements.**

Keywords-Solid-state sensor; Compton Computed tomography; compaction measurements; agricultural sensor; intelligent instrumentation; soil analysis.

I. INTRODUCTION

Nowadays, sensor-based technologies have emerged for use and investigation on several domains of application.

In the field of tomographic imaging the progress in sensors has been leading many scientists, engineers, and technicians to present additional interest and to devote greater time to their activities.

This has been enlarging the world evolution for decision support systems, which are sensors-technology based. Such aspects, have also expanded economy, i.e., with additional opportunities for many fields of interest, like medical [1], industrial [2], and agricultural [3], among others.

X and γ-ray Computed Tomography (CT) was born with contributions from both the physicist Allan MacLeod Cormack and engineer Godfrey Newbold Hounsfield [4][5]. Later, Cormack came to know the work of the Austrian mathematician Johann Radon [6], who was the first to present a general mathematical solution for the reconstruction of a body from its projections in a space of order (n) that is, enabling the determination of a density function of a studied region through its projections. In fact, Cormack has developed equations to reconstruct an area considering a finite number of projections. Also, he defined a density function, based on the mass attenuation coefficients (cm^2/g), and used back-projection to obtain photon attenuation measurements based on the Beer-Lambert equation [7].

In 1979, Cormack and Hounsfield shared the Nobel Prize in Medicine, due their innovative work based on X-ray tomograph. In this context, it is also important to mention, as important contribution for such a result the pioneering works carried out by Michael Faraday (1831) and Wilhelm Conrad Röntgen (1895). Michael Faraday was one of the first to study the relationship between electricity and magnetism. He discovered, in 1831, that electromagnetic induction and his studies are considered key concepts in current physics, finding applications in several areas including tomography. In 1895, Wilhelm Conrad Röntgen produced and detected electromagnetic radiation in different wavelengths, which he came to call X-rays.

There are different instrumental arrangements based on the interaction of the ionizing energies with matter, which defines the operational modalities for the X and γ-ray tomographs. Here, we are considering two of these approaches, i.e., one based on the transmission and other related to the scattered photons. Transmission tomography uses a collimated beam of radiation, which defines planes as thin as the beam itself and, through several parallel collimated beams, sets of projections can be defined that are taken to image reconstruction algorithms.

In fact, the study of CT applied to agriculture, has begun in the early 1980s, primarily based on transmission tomography and focused on the investigation of water content (cm^3/cm^3), soil density and compaction (g/cm^3), as well as soil porosity (%).

The first customized X and γ-ray minitomograph scanner for soil science applications was built in 1987 [8]. Subsequently, other agricultural tomographs were developed to operate at millimeter scale, i.e., considering either photons transmission or scattering techniques [9-13].

Based on scattering photons technique, the Compton effect was first presented by Compton and Hagenow [14][15].

In fact, conventional transmission tomography techniques and conventional tomography models are based on the use of source and detector on opposite sides. When used appropriately, the benefits of a CT scan far exceed the risks. CT scans can provide detailed information to soil diagnose. Additionally, the detailed images provided by CT scans may decrease the need for agricultural machinery uses for soil management. However, these models cannot always be used in agricultural applications, such as, for example, in extracting soil measurements directly from either an agricultural field or crop area.

The Compton scattering tomograph has source and detector located on the same side in relation to the sample of interest to be sampled. In this way, there is no need to open trenches for soil analysis, as necessary when using the transmission tomographic technique.

In such field of knowledge, Hanson and Gigante have developed a mathematical method to visualize the scattering geometry of the energy distribution and the angular variation of the Compton scattering [16][17]. However, these authors considered the absorption effects to be very small and obtained toroidal surfaces of constant angle and correspondent energies for scattering. Additionally, they emphasized the importance of observing energy contours within a scattered volume, as these determined the magnitude of geometric effects. They also have shown that this type of analysis would be useful as an analytical approach to measurements with X-rays using scattered photons. Besides, it was important to understand the Compton´s photopeak in order to obtain accurate measurements.

In 1992, Cesareo and coauthors published an article on the theoretical basis and applications in techniques that used the interaction of photons with matter considered a broad keV energy range [18]. Analytical applications included Compton densitometry, Compton profile measurements, and Rayleigh scattering to Compton scattering (R/C) ratio measurements. Regarding Compton densitometry, the authors emphasized that this method of analysis can be used to determine the electronic density of the sample, but not its mass density, which can be deduced by knowing the value of the relation regarding the atomic number to the effective atomic mass of the sample, i.e., the (Z/A) ratio.

About the Compton profile measurements, they reported that the technique was considered an important source of information about the modifications of the electron moment distributions in the sample. However, the technique had difficulties in measurements due multispectral incident beam energy and the multiple scattering occurrences. Regarding the (R/C) ratio measurement, the authors reported works that make such measures feasible.

Balogun and Spyrou investigated the influence that materials with high and low atomic number Z exerted on CCT images [19]. These authors used a 662 keV (^{137}Cs) γ-ray source with a rectangular collimator, a Phantom consisting of a cylindrical aluminum (Al) block with 52 mm in diameter and 5 holes arranged in a circle. Two of these holes were 1.2 cm in diameter, while the others were in the range of 5 and 6 cm in diameter.

The holes were made to insert rods whose chemical composition would be of interest to the research. They justified this type of arrangement based on the analysis of the contrast and the signal-to-noise ratio (SNR) evaluation. Such analysis has considered an expectation about 60% in contrast for reconstructed images from a Phantom having diverse materials. The best results for contrast, SNR and accuracy were obtained with the inclusion of Lead (Pb, high Z) and Cooper (Cu, low Z) in the Phantom, and the author's hypothesis have been proved successfully. Likewise, the minimum detectable change in bulk density was equal to 4.2 g/cm^3.

In 1994, Norton developed a technique for tomographic images reconstructing through the number of scattered photons as a function of energy and detector positioning [20]. The result obtained was an electron density image that could be reconstructed by measuring its line integrals over various paths. This result presented an analytical solution for the idealized Compton image reconstruction problem. Norton emphasized that the back-projection method had the advantage of being computationally efficient compared to methods based on numerical systems of equations. Additionally, the author stated that such a solution was based on the use of Monte Carlo method, i.e., has been found iteratively.

This paper presents the use of an embedded X and γ-ray high-performance detector in a Compton scattering tomograph, customized for agricultural soil compaction evaluations on the crop's region. After this introduction, there are Section II, which presents advances in the use of such a technique in agriculture, and Section III with material and methods, considering the main aspects. In addition, there is Section IV with results and discussions, and finally, the conclusions are presented in Section V.

II. Early use of Compton Scattering Tomograph in Agriculture

The scattering tomography, known as Compton Computed Tomography (CCT), has being used for imaging reconstruction from projections of agricultural soils.

In fact, Cruvinel and Balogun have developed a dual-energy Compton scattering tomograph for agricultural applications [21][22]. The experimental setup consisted of two radioactive sources, one of 662 keV (^{137}Cs) for soil density measurements and another of 59.6 keV (^{231}Am) for soil water content measurements with 2 mm spatial resolution. In such publications, these authors have also presented a deep discussion regarding the comparison with other methodologies, as well as advantages for soil density and water content measurements based on CCT. In such a context, they have shown a linear relationship between the size of soil aggregates and the Compton measurements with a regression coefficient (r^2) better than 0.95 for bulk density and 0.70 for water content.

The minimum density detected was 0.13 g/cm^3, i.e., with an accuracy of 2%. Besides, the minimum value of the water content detected was about 0.10 cm^3/cm^3, i.e., with an accuracy of 5%. In 2003, these same authors have presented the use of a NaI(Tl) scintillation detector and the qualification of the use of a photopeak in the region of 250 keV to carry out Compton measurements (Fig. 1). In such a research work, the Compton images obtained showed good resolution contrast, shape and edge definition.

Additionally, they reported that in Compton scattering photon tomography the choice of scattering energy was dictated by the scattering angle, materials to be examined and the size or depth of the sample. For soil analysis, the use of low energy photons ($\lesssim$ 60 keV) was indicated for studies of surface phenomena, such as soil sealing. In situations that require depth information, such as soil compaction, higher energy photons would favor the analysis.

In 2004, Roy and Pratt compared Klein-Nishina cross-section measurements for the whole atom (energy range from 11 keV to 40 keV) with the theory and used a synchrotron-type X-ray source [23]. Compton scattering measurements were performed with a scattering angle equal to 90°. The results showed experimental comparison of the cross sections measured with conventional and synchrotron sources with the predicted values of the Compton scattering factor, that means, an Incoherent Scattering Factor (ISF). The measurements made with conventional sources were presented in a dispersed way, having a difference in the magnitude of the ISF in the range of 5% to 50%, while the measurements with the synchrotron fell in a narrow range of low percentage of difference. The authors highlighted the need for studies on Compton scattering measurements in the region below 10 keV in order to confirm the adequacy of the theoretical treatment.

In 2009, Yao and Leszczynski presented an analytical approach to approximately separate the unknown information from the Klein-Nishina cross-section formula and express it through the primary intensity of X-rays in the detector [24]. These authors reported that the spatial distribution of the first order Compton scattered could be described by the Klein-Nishina cross section formula assuming that the source energy spectrum, the geometry of the imaging system and the volumetric information of the scattering medium were known, including geometry and radiation distribution properties. Such information was mixed up and generally could not be completely separated. The authors also considered an approximate formula in which characteristics were separated from the information from the X-ray source and the imaging system. The approximation obtained was compared with the exact solution of the Klein-Nishina cross section and with the simulations carried out using the Monte Carlo method. The result obtained showed that the approximate relationship between the first order scattering and the fluence of the primary intensity in the detector was useful in estimating the scattered radiation in physical projections of a specimen.

In 2010, Pratt and co-authors reviewed the standard theory on Compton scattering of valence electrons and described findings that required modification of the usual understanding by looking at the consequences for the experiment [25]. In such a work, the authors demonstrated that the estimate made by Eisenberg and Platzman for the validity of the impulse approximation theory and its application to Compton scattering was incorrect, although the qualitative conclusion remained intact. They pointed out that the impulse approximation provided a good description of Compton scattering in the peak region, but failed when considering low-energy resulting photons.

In 2011, Şahin and collaborators measured water retention in soils using Compton scattering. The experimental arrangement used a γ-ray source 133Ba (500 mCi, 356 keV) and a NaI(Tl) scintillator detector [26]. The soil used was a Holocene or Fluvial Neosol (Entisol) according to the North American classification (USA).

Additionally, the chosen spreading angle was 90° and the soil thickness varied from 5 to 55 mm with a 5 mm pitch. The mass attenuation coefficient value obtained was 0.102 cm^2/g and the relationship between the amount of water added and the intensity of scattered radiation showed a correlation coefficient (r^2) equal to 0.99. The authors concluded that the performance of the method with Compton scattering based on the standard curve showed that the results obtained from the evaluation of the analytical uncertainties were satisfactory.

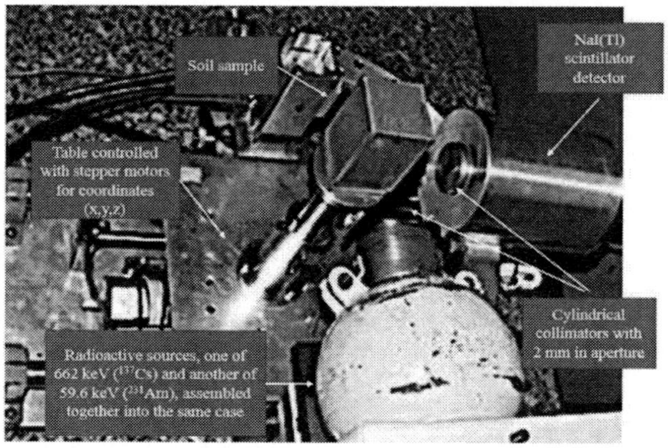

Figure 1. Laboratory version of the Compton CT scanner for agricultural soil and water analyzes [21].

In 2011, Cruvinel and Scannavino Junior have published an instrumental evolution on Compton scattering, i.e., the development of a field densitometer that uses an X-ray source and digital signal processing to measure the soil density of arable soils [27].

In recent times, one may find progress in agriculture technologies, that means, in terms of the use of sensor-based techniques for soil analysis. In fact, either nom-ionizing or ionizing radiations have been used, and challenges are still related to decrease invasiveness of the measure probes for data acquisition, as well as improvements in accuracy and precision of the measurements.

Furthermore, also improvements have been required in computational models to help decision-making directly on farm [28-31]. Likewise, the intelligent agriculture industry is expanding quickly, bringing and presenting new solutions to the farmers practically daily.

III. MATERIALS AND METHODS

Considering the CCT's instrumentation for soil analysis (Fig. 2), the detector positioning is established from the selection of the scattering angle, which determines the Klein-Nishina cross section and the energy of the scattered photons. Besides, the collimators diameters of the source and detector, together with their lengths, determine the aperture half-angles that influence the intersection volume of the field of view established between source and detector.

From a Compton process the scattered photons number (dS) can be observed by equation (1), which shows the contributions of the linear attenuation coefficients, both for the incidence (μ_1) and scattering energy (μ_2), as well as the Klein-Nishina differential cross section ($d\sigma^{KN}/d\Omega$). Then, in order to account for these, we can write, for the number of singly scattered photons detected at the detector during a counting time of (t) seconds:

$$dS = \varphi_0 \exp\left(^{\int_{x1}\mu_1 dx}\right)\frac{d\sigma^{KN}}{d\Omega}\rho \\ .\frac{N_A Z \xi t}{A}\exp\left(^{\int_{x2}\mu_2 dx}\right) dV d\Omega \qquad (1)$$

where exponential factors are introduced to take care of the attenuation of the primary and scattered photons within the sample, (ξ) is the detector's photopeak counting efficiency at the scattered photon energy, (x1) and (x2) represent the photon's path lengths in the sample, from the source to the scattering center and back to the detector, respectively, (ϕ_0) is the incident photon flux of energy (E_0), (ρ) the soil bulk density, (A) the mass number, and (N_A) is the Avogadro's number.

Furthermore, a commercially available Silicon-Drift-Detector (SDD) was used in such instrumental arrangement [32-34]. The performance of the SDD can be observed in Fig. 3, i.e., efficiency versus energy. The SDD sensor used in this study has a discrete external Field Effect Transistor (FET) and it uses a dedicated feedback capacitor and a well-proven method of pulsed charge restoration. This allows stability and provide more accurate X and γ-ray measurement.

In addition, as part of the used methods, the Filtered Back-projection Algorithm (FBP) was also considered [35][36]. In fact, the tomographic image reconstruction is a process to estimate a slice f(x,y) image from a set of projections p(t,θ). In such application, each sampled point of each projection collected at angle (θ) is correspondent to the scanned scattered photons intensity for one of the geographical positions of the sampled region. The basis of the mathematical model for the Compton`s image reconstruction can be such a reconstruction algorithm. The FBP algorithm is often referred as the convolution method using a one-dimensional integral equation for the reconstruction of a two-dimensional image. This method is the most common reconstruction algorithm used today for CT application. It uses projections and their Fourier Transform (FT), i.e., considering Q(w) as the filtered $P_\theta(t)$ projection. To get the reconstructed image, the resulting projections for different angles (θ_i) are added to estimate f(x,y). The reconstruction model can be presented, in its discrete form, as follows.

$$f(x,y) = \frac{\pi}{K}\sum_{i=1}^{k} Q_{\theta i}(x cos\theta_i + y sen\theta_i) \qquad (2)$$

where (K) represents the numbers of the interval of angles (θ_i) during the scanning process.

The interface with the user is performed by a computer algorithm developed for communication between the control system and the SDD data acquisition, and it is also able to reconstructed the CCT images.

Besides, the algorithm allows to organize tasks to receive and collected data of soil compaction and in organizing an image bank for future use and analyzes, i.e., interpretation of spatial variability of soil compaction in A-horizon of the soil landscape.

For validation, a databank of soil CCT images were obtained considering an experimental agricultural plot, located at the geographic coordinates 21°57'13.9"S and 47°51'10.9"W, i.e., at the National Laboratory of Precision Agriculture (LANAPRE) in São Carlos, SP, Brazil.

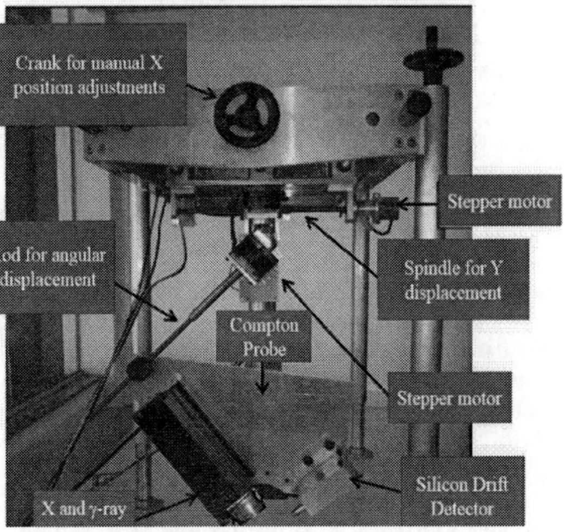

Figure 2. Instrumentation and probe of the customized and portable Compton scattering tomograph for soil compaction analysis.

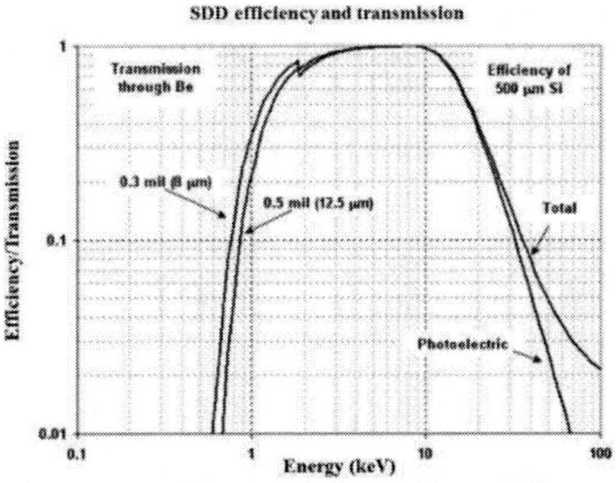

Figure 3. Efficiency versus energy for the SDD.

The mechanical module of the CCT is composed of a XYZ table for the spatial localization of the measurement Compton`s probe for soil compaction. The XYZ table is sustained by fuses and linear shafts of dislocation over the support structure. The imaging area of the CCT allows to image a Region of Interest (ROI) equal to 1.0 m x 0.50 m. It is sustained by three adjustable legs, with two at each frame extremity and one that is centralized on the opposite side to facilitate the entire leveling of the structure.

IV. RESULTS AND DISCUSSION

The used SDD is a state-of-the-art semiconductor detector based on the principle of side-ward depletion. When it was customized to be used in the CCT a comparison has been made with the measuring obtained with a NaI(Tl) scintillation detector. As an observed result, the SDD has presented advantages in comparison to the use of a NaI(Tl) detector. Such a comparison is summarized in Table I.

TABLE I. COMPARATIVE RESULTS FOR THE DETECTORS VARIABLES

Detector Characteristics	NaI(Tl) scintillation	SDD
Effective area (mm^2)	16	100
Thickness (mm)	76.2	0.26
Energy resolution (FWHM) @ 662keV (keV)	46.3	16.5
Signal-to-Noise ratio (SNR)	4	83

It is observed that, the energy resolution for 662 keV gamma rays is a function the workable temperature of the SDD, when considering the shaping time constants equal to 0.5 and 1 μ s. It was also observed that cooling reduces noise contribution. Nevertheless, an acceptable energy resolution is obtained up to SDD temperatures around 50 °C, which is useful for agricultural field use. Figure 4 shows the CCT working region evaluated for the SDD.

A calibration curve for the pixel value in ($kg.m^{-3}$) was carried out by using a set of well-known soil samples and a conventional penetrometer.

Figure 5 shows, as one example, a 100 mm x 50 mm Compton image from the organized databank. It was collected for analysis from the agricultural experimental field. In such a result the pixel is equal to 2.5 mm^2, and the total amount of pixels per image is equal to 800 (20x40). The source energy used was equal to 662 keV (^{137}Cs). The total amount of time to collect all projections and to have a final Compton image reconstructed was equal to 30 minutes.

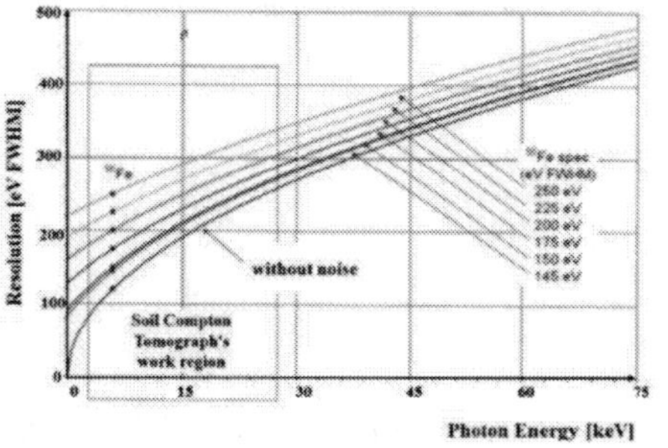

Figure 4. The CCT working region evaluated for the SDD based on 145 eV resolution.

For a given collimator size, length, and, its distance from the scattering center, scattering volume increases with increasing angle in the back-scattering geometry. The best volume resolution was found within the 90°±5° scattering angle range. Though volume resolution also decreases towards the forward scattering angles, resolution rate loss is much more pronounced in the backscatter angles.

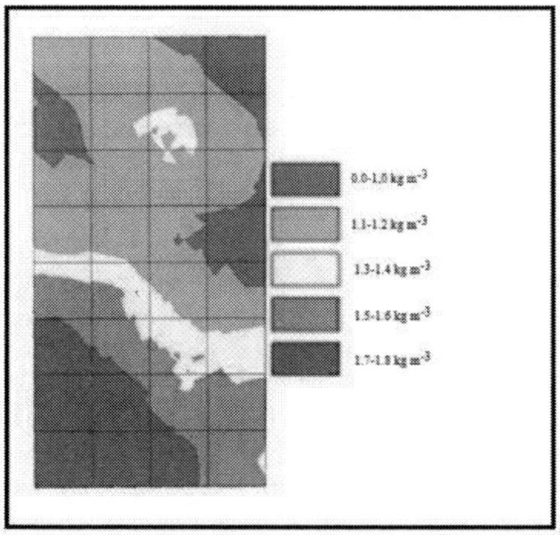

Figure 5. An example of Compton image from the agricultural pilot. The pseudo-color scale is calibrated in ($kg.m^{-3}$) and represents the soil compaction presented in the scanned area. From the grid used over the image one may have 25 pixels per block.

The use of CCT has enabled non-invasive analysis of the interior of the agricultural soil. Therefore, it has allowed the evaluation in situ of the A-horizon into an experimental area, as well as the information about its spatial soil compaction variability.

Soil compaction can have both desirable and undesirable effects on plant growth. A slightly compacted soil can speed up the rate of seed germination because it promotes good seed-to-soil contact. In fact, as soil compaction increases beyond optimum, yields begin to decline. In dry years, soil compaction can lead to stunted, drought-stressed plants due to decreased root growth. Without timely rains and well-placed fertilizers, yields will reduce.

In wet weather, yields decrease with any increase in compaction. Soil compaction in wet years decreases soil aeration, increasing denitrification. All these factors add stress to the crop and lead to yield loss, i.e., favoring food insecurity.

V. CONCLUSION

We have carried out studies related to the application of the SDD, and started its use in a customized Compton scattering tomograph for agricultural applications. The physics aspects of such a detector, that includes a solid-state based-sensor, was also evaluated for its well operation and functioning. Besides, result have shown advantages when using the SSD in comparison with a NaI(Tl) detector, since it presented good energy resolution, high SNR, as well as suppression of the Compton background. Further, an agricultural validation was considered using a set of Compton images for evaluating the spatial variability of soil compaction in $kg.m^{-3}$. In fact, such a result has proved to be possible non-invasive analysis of the compaction level of agricultural soil layers, directly on the field. For the future, it is planning to include a soil moisture sensor with the Compton probe, as well as to use algorithm to support decision making to orient agricultural machinery in precision soil compactness corrections.

ACKNOWLEDGMENT

This research was partially supported by the Brazilian Corporation for Agricultural Research (Embrapa).

REFERENCES

[1] H. Jung, "Basic physical principles and clinical applications of computed tomography", Progress in Medical Physics, vol. 32, no. 1, pp. 1-17, 2021.

[2] U. Hampel et al. "A review on fast tomographic imaging techniques and their potential application in industrial process control", Sensors, pp. 2309-2331, 2022.

[3] T. Kim et al. "Comparison of X-ray computed tomography and magnetic resonance imaging to detect pest-infested fruits: A pilot study", Nuclear Engineering and Technology, vol. 54, no. 2, pp. 514-522, 2022.

[4] A. M. Cormack, "Representation of a foundation by Its Line with some radiological application". Journal of Applied Physics, vol. 34, n. 9, pp. 2722-2727, 1963.

[5] G. N. Hounsfield, "Computerized transverse axial scanning (tomography). 1. description of system", British Journal of Radiology, vol. 46, pp. 1016-1022, 1973.

[6] J. Radon, "About the determination of functions by their integral values along certain manifolds", (Original in Germany: Über die Bestimmung von Funktionen durch ihre Integralwerte längs gewisser Mannigfaltigkeiten). In: Proceedings... Royal Saxonian Academy of Sciences at Leipzig, Mathematical and Physical Section, vol. 69, pp. 262–277, 1917.

[7] D. F. Swinehart, "The Beer-Lambert Law", Journal of Chemical Education, vol. 39, pp. 7-333, 1962.

[8] P. E. Cruvinel, R. Cesareo, S. Crestana, and S. Mascarenhas, "X-and gamma-rays computerized minitomograph scanner for soil science", IEEE Transactions on Instrumentation and Measurement, vol. 39, n. 5, pp. 745–750, 1990.

[9] Á. Macedo et al. "Wood density determination by X and gamma ray tomography", International Journal of the Biology, Chemistry, Physics and Technology of Wood, vol. 56, pp. 535–540, 2002.

[10] A. Pedrotti et al. "Computed tomography applied to studies of a planosoil" (Original in Portuguese: Tomografia computadorizada aplicada a estudos de um planossolo). Brazilian Agricultural Research Journal, vol. 38, n. 7, pp. 819–826, Brazil, 2003.

[11] P.E. Cruvinel, M. L. F. Pereira, J. H. Saito, and L.F. Costa, "Performance optimization of tomographic image reconstruction based on DSP processors", IEEE Transactions on Instrumentation and Measurement , vol. 58, pp. 3295-3304, 2009.

[12] J. M. Beraldo, F. A. Scanavinno Junior, and P. E. Cruvinel, "Application of X-ray computed tomography in the evaluation of soil porosity in soil management systems", Engenharia Agrícola, vol. 34, n. 6, pp. 1162–1174, 2014.

[13] M. F. L. Pereira and P. E. Cruvinel, "A model for soil computed tomography based on volumetric reconstruction, Wiener filtering and parallel processing", Computers and Electronics In Agriculture, vol. 111, pp. 151-163, 2015.

[14] A. H. Compton, "A Quantum Theory of the Scattering of X-rays by Light Elements", Physics Review, vol. 21, pp. 483-502, 1923.

[15] A. H. Compton and C. F. Hagenow, "A measurement of the polarization of secondary X-rays. Journal of the Optical Society of America and review of scientific instruments, vol. 8, pp. 487-491, 1924.

[16] A. L. Hanson, G. E. Gigante, and M. Meron, "Contours of constant scattering angle", Physical Review Letters, vol. 61, n. 2, pp. 135-137, 1988.

[17] A. L. Hanson and G. E. Gigante, "Evaluation of geometrical contributions to the spread of the Compton-scatter energy distribution", Physical Review A, vol. 40, n. 1, pp. 171-180, 1989.

[18] R. Cesareo et al. "Interaction of keV photons with matter and new applications", Physics Reports, vol. 213, n. 3, pp. 117-178, 1992.

[19] F. A. Balogun and N. M. Spyrou, "Compton scattering tomography in the study of a dense inclusion in a lighter matrix", Nuclear Instruments and Methods in Physics Research B, vol. 83, n. 4, pp. 533-538, 1993.

[20] S. J. Norton, "Compton scattering tomography", Journal of Applied Physics, vol. 76, n. 4, pp. 2007-2015, 1994.

[21] P. E. Cruvinel and F. A. Balogun, "Minitomography scanner for agriculture based on dual-energy Compton scattering", In: Brazilian Symposium on Computer Graphics and Image Processing-SIBGRAPI, Proceedings... Los Alamitos: IEEE Computer Society, pp. 193-199, 2000.

[22] P. E. Cruvinel and F. A. Balogun, "Compton scattering tomography for agricultural measurements" Journal of the Brazilian Association of Agricultural Engineering, vol. 26, n. 1, pp. 151-160, 2006.

[23] S. C. Roy and R. H. Pratt, " Need for further inelastic scattering measurements at X-ray energies", Radiation Physics and Chemistry, vol. 69, pp. 193-197, 2004.

[24] W. Yao and K. Leszczynski, "An analytical approach to estimating the first order X-ray scatter in heterogeneous medium", Medical Physics, vol. 36, n. 7, pp. 3145-3156, 2009.

[25] R. H. Pratt et al. "Compton scattering revisited", Radiation Physics and Chemistry, vol. 79, pp. 124-131, 2010.

[26] Y. Şahin et al. "Measurement of soil water using Compton scattering", X-Ray pectrometry", vol. 40, n. 4, pp. 315-318, 2011.

[27] P. E. Cruvinel and F. A. Scannavino Junior, "Evolution of an instrument for evaluating the compaction of agricultural soils with Compton scattering", (Original in Portuguese: Evolução de um instrumento para avaliação da compactação de solos agrícolas com espalhamento Compton), In: Congresso Brasileiro de Engenharia Agrícola – CONBEA, vol 40, n. TR0713, 2011.

[28] A. Kaloxylos et al. "Farm management systems and the future internet era", Computers and Electronics in Agriculture, vol. 89, pp. 130– 144, 2012.

[29] Y. Sato et al. "Remote radiation imaging system using a compact gamma-ray imager mounted on a multicopter drone", Journal of Nuclear Science and Technology, vol. 55, pp. 90–96, 2018.

[30] A. Plasencia, Y. Shichkina, I. Suárez, and Z. Ruiz, "Open source robotic simulators platforms for teaching deep reinforcement learning algorithms", Procedia Computer Science, vol. 150, pp. 162–170, 2019.

[31] O. Gonzalez et al. "Development and assessment of a tractor driving simulator with immersive virtual reality for training to avoid occupational hazards", Computers and Electronics in Agriculture, vol. 143, pp. 111-118, 2017.

[32] E. Gatti and P. Rehak P, "Semiconductor drift chamber — An application of a novel charge transport scheme", Nuclear Instruments and Methods A, vol. 225, pp. 608 – 614, 1984.

[33] P. Lechner et al. "Silicon drift detectors for high resolution, high count rate x-ray spectroscopy at room temperature, Nuclear Instruments and Methods A, vol. 458, pp. 281–287, 2001.

[34] L. Wang et al. "Design and fabrication of quasi-double-sided silicon drift detector for x-ray detection", Materials Science in Semiconductor Processing, vol.155, n. 1, pp. 107201, 2023.

[35] Oppenheim, A.V., and R.W. Schafer, "Discrete-Time Signal Processing", Prentice-Hall, Hoboken,1989.

[36] J. Hsieh, "Computed Tomography: Principles, Design, Artifacts, and Recent Advances", Wiley, New York, 2nd ed, 2009.

Strategy for the Deployment of Water Internet of Things (WIoT) in Taiwan

*Chen-Yang Hsu, Shu-Yi Peng, Chen-Hua Chu, Fan-Lun Chen
Green Energy and Environment Research Laboratories
Industrial Technology Research Institute, Hsinchu, Taiwan
e-mail: ambrosehsu@itri.org.tw

Abstract—According to the advancement of information networks and sensing technology, the Internet of Things (IoT) is the new trend of future technology and information. In view of the increasing maturity of water quality sensor technology and the rapid advancement of information and communication technology in recent years. Previously, water quality sampling required a lot of labor and expensive equipment for data collection. This study has developed water quality sensor component installations in areas with potential water pollution. Establishing Taiwan's water quality sensing system through a sensor connecting network monitoring Taiwan's water environment and using a solution framework, and 4 strategies to lay the foundation for the development of smart cities.

Keywords- Internet Of Things; Water Quality Sensing; Pollution Hotspots; Pollution Source Tracking; Environmental Governance

I. INTRODUCTION

In Taiwan, the water quality and environmental testing relies on a large amount of manpower to collect samples manually. The Taiwanese administration utilizes the "Sampling Unit" and then send them to the "Testing Unit" for testing with laboratory standard instruments. If it is confirmed that the pollutant exceeds the standard, the "remediation unit" will control the environment, and if it is confirmed that there was a pollution violation, the "environmental enforcement unit" of the government will inspect and punish the illegal manufacturer [1].

The above mentioned existing environmental testing industry is quite time-consuming and labor-intensive, and the time and spatial resolution of the monitoring data is insufficient, making it rather difficult to grasp the trend of water quality changes at any time and affecting the timeliness of back-end environmental governance and environmental enforcement.

Environmental quality gradually gains awareness of practitioners. The usage of big data to achieve environmental governance, real-time monitoring, protection of water quality by early warning, response to abnormal situations, and to provide efficient solutions have become the next stage of environmental governance trend amongst Taiwan's smart cities [2].

II. COMPREHENSIVE WATER SENSING PLAN

In recent years, online water quality analysis and sampling technologies have become increasingly sophisticated. With the advancement of data analysis, big data processing, and wireless transmission technologies, Environmental Protection Administration (EPA) Taiwan has established a set of total solutions for the environmental pollution monitoring ecosystem including the environmental survey, environmental sampling, environmental inspection, environmental remediation, and environmental enforcement. The use of smart sensing of high-resolution water quality spatial and temporal data, low-cost sensing equipment, big data analysis, and automatic control completes the last piece of the environmental pollution monitoring ecosystem (See Figure 1).

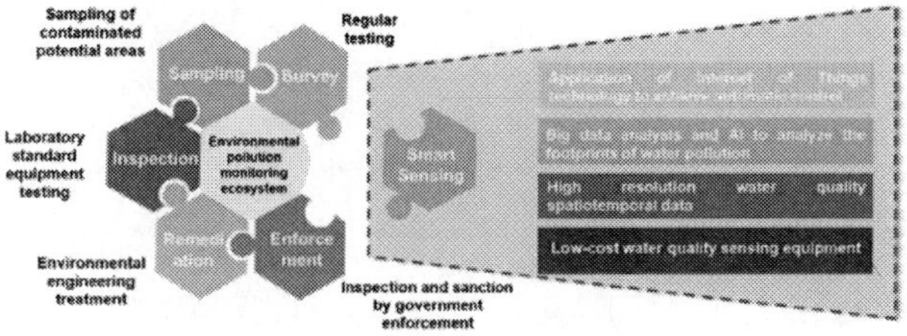

Figure 1. WIoT Smart Monitoring Map

With the widely distribution of Water Quality IoT (WIoT) sensors in Taiwan, it allows us to monitor the characteristics of water quality and background concentration of the sensing area all day. From environmental information disclosure to environmental governance, water quality monitoring and management applications are implemented to reduce the manpower required by the environmental protection bureaus in counties and municipalities, effectively improving environmental quality.

III. METHODS AND SOLUTION

The objective of this study was to investigate the establishment of the WIoT Data Analysis System and miniaturized water quality monitoring system device for the purpose of monitoring water quality in Taiwan.

A. *Miniaturized water quality monitoring system device*

Compared with the traditional water quality measurement equipment, the new generation of WIoT sensors are highly mobile and can be quickly installed for applications. There are two usages of fixed-point sensing and drifting downstream, which have the following benefits: easy to operate, low setup-cost, and come with wireless data transmission. (See Figure 2)

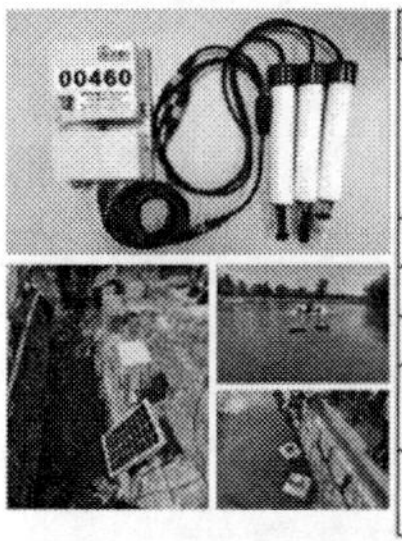

Item	Details
Sensor Categories	pH : 0 – 14 (±0.1 pH) EC : 300-4000 μS/cm (±15%) DO : ±1.0mg/L Temp : ±0.5℃
Detection Frequency	1 minute
Size	215*160*62.5
Communications	GSM/LoRa
Applicable Environments	River Water, Irrigation Water, Factory Discharge Areas
Features	Swift Analysis, Small footprint, Low Power Consumption, Affordable Price

Figure 2. Water Quality Monitoring System

The measuring items include pH, EC, Temp., and dissolved oxygen. This method can be widely extended to various fields of measurement applications, such as factory outfalls, potentially polluted agricultural land, aquaculture, rivers, sewage drains, water purification plants, etc. With rapid deployment and its low-cost, it can assist standard large monitoring stations to achieve the benefits of point and line sensing in water networks.

B. Water Quality IoT (WIoT) Data Analysis System

In order to maximize the effects of online water quality monitoring, this study designed a solution framework suitable for an IoT water quality monitoring network (See Figure 3).

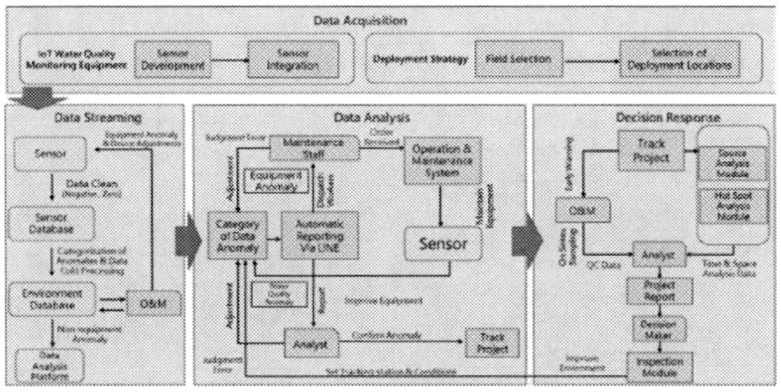

Figure 3. WIoT Monitoring And Management Framework

The purposes of the framework are as flows: (1) Establish a systematic structure of water quality environmental governance. (2) Automate the tracking of data analysis. (3) Standardize the management of abnormal water quality incidents. This framework suggests systematic processes for obtaining data, streaming, and analyzing back-end decision-making and response measures. At the data acquisition end, appropriate IoT water quality monitoring devices must be selected depending on the purpose of monitoring. Also, a deployment strategy must be implemented to include suitable installation locations. Such mechanism ensures all acquired data can satisfy the purpose of monitoring [3].

IV. Discussion

EPA Taiwan is committed to promote the WIoT. With the development of component research and development, field deployment, data analysis, and value-added application. EPA Taiwan is aiming to deploy 170 self-developed water quality monitoring devices by 2023 to control the quality of water bodies and trace the source of pollution discharge.

The comprehensive smart water quality monitoring system (See Figure 4) can also be expanded into the field of agricultural, industrial, and livelihood, such as industrial wastewater pollution sensing, potential pollution source sensing, smart aquaculture, agricultural water safety, irrigation water sensing, watergate switching, smart sewage treatment and control, and drinking water sensing, etc. In the future, with the gradual increase of demand, it is expected to drive the overall environmental IoT industry chain and create emerging markets.

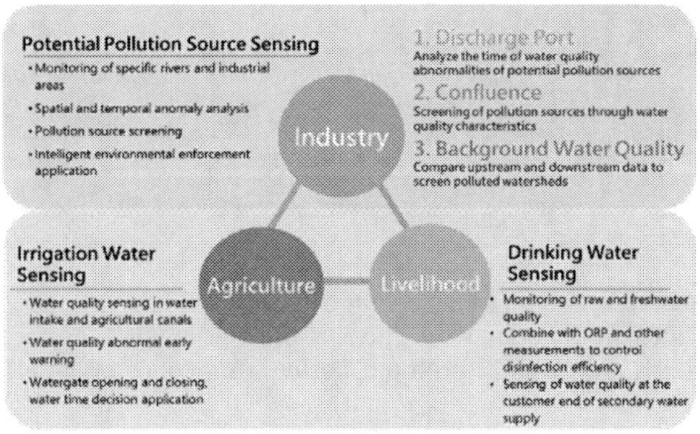

Figure 4. Application Scenarios

Water quality data analysis model could achieve the goals such as prediction and early warning, pollution traceability, hot zone analysis, etc. The establishment of WIoT environmental governance program enables analysis of water quality data characteristics, combined with cross-sector data analysis, it can determine the hot zone of water pollution and achieve upstream traceability and downstream warning.

A. Selecting Monitoring Stations

The source of the pollution analysis model consists of 3 components including the decision support system (DSS) layer, the data layer, and other data connections. When the water quality sensors detect anomalies and issue early warnings, companies located in upstream areas of pollution are immediately identified to reduce the scope of the investigation and increase emergency response capability (See Figure 5).

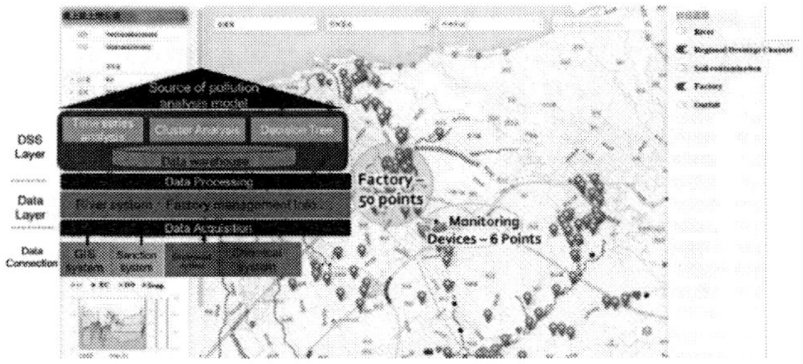

Figure 5. Pollution Source Analysis Module

Monitoring stations that require further analysis are selected based on analysis models of the automatic continuous monitoring and early warning system. The system utilizes Geographic Information System (GIS) analysis functionality to screen sections of the river close to the station. With this, users can confirm whether they would like to change the scope of analysis.

B. Screening By Industry

By default, the system filters factories with high pollution potentials within a 5-km radius of the monitoring station. Users can categorize the data by industry based on the type of pollution, such as Printed Circuit Board (PCB) manufacturing. The system will present an industry list that includes factory names, locations, and addresses on the GIS graphical layer that can be selected and added to the analysis list.

C. Materials And Audit Data Analysis

The system filters factories according to Step B to further analyze their basic data, status of material registration, and past results from the previous audits. Searches can be conducted on their latest data related to water pollution, waste, punitive actions, and registration status in the last 3 years.

D. Pollution Hotspot Analysis Model

The purpose of this model is to measure the degree of impact by water pollution in downstream areas to achieve the critical task of quickly evaluating early warnings. The purpose of this model is to measure the degree of impact by water pollution in downstream areas to achieve the critical task of quickly evaluating early warnings. There are 5 problems promptly following: (1) the time for pollution to reach sensitive downstream areas; (2) the amount of maximum pollution concentration; (3) the total area of pollution; and (4) the duration of pollution concentration; (5) the time that pollution would exceed the safety limitation.

V. Conclusions And Future Work

Varied from traditional monitoring, this study utilizes WIoT technology to obtain a large amount of data, which are then used to build new water quality application models, including an alert model and forecast model, through the widespread deployment of sensors.

To achieve early warning according to data anomalies, upstream pollution source tracking, and downstream pollution hotspot prediction, the deployment of large-scale is essential to obtain spatial and temporal high-resolution monitoring data and integrated data from multiple regions with the help of data analysis models.

This study has deployed more than 100 miniaturized water quality monitoring devices and successfully applied the data analysis model to identify cases of data anomalies in water quality for law enforcement. These devices were installed in various locations in Taiwan with potential water pollution, and data collected from the devices has transmitted to a centralized database for analysis.

The data analysis model developed in this study was applied to identify cases of data anomalies in water quality for law enforcement. This allowed authorities to quickly identify and response to cases of water pollution and improve the overall environmental quality of the affected areas.

The successful deployment and application of the data analysis model in this case study validated the recommendations made in this study, proving that miniaturized water quality monitoring equipment can be effectively utilized for early warning and pollution control.

In the future, we will continue to promote the application of WIoT monitoring system in wastewater treatment monitoring (or more) through the field of industrial, medical, and the general public. WIoT equipment can set up early water-quality warning module at the monitoring stations and the adjust the process and treatment unit in real time by analyzing the change of historical data. With the cooperation between government policies, big data analysis models, and the usage of machine learning, they can provide early warnings and smart control functions that would continue to further perfect Taiwan's IoT industry chain.

References

[1] Allan IJ, Vrana B, Greenwood R, Mills GA, Roig B, Gonzalez C. "A "toolbox" for biological and chemical monitoring requirements for the European Union's Water Framework Directive," Talanta. 2006 Apr 15;69(2):302-22.

[2] C. C. Tsai, F. L Chen, and B. C Yang, "Solve the problem of smart innovation and joyful city," IEK Industry News Network: How to enhance the dynamic of an ecological environment with intelligent perception, pp.30

[3] F. L Chen, B. C Yang, S. Y. Peng, and T. C. Lin, "Applying a deployment strategy and data analysis model for water quality continuous monitoring and management," International Journal of Distributed Sensor Networks 2020, Vol. 16(6)